YOUR FIRST 90 DAYS
MANAGING PEOPLE

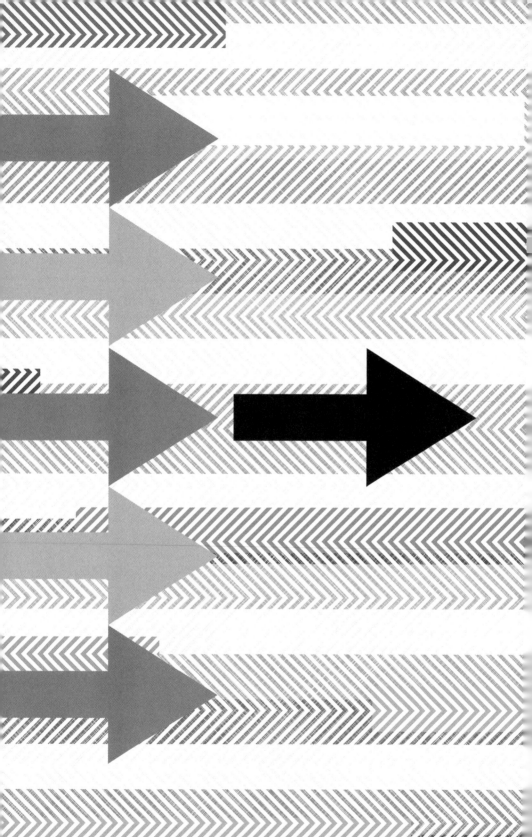

YOUR FIRST 90 DAYS

Managing People

A NEW MANAGER'S GUIDE TO IMPACTFUL LEADERSHIP

DR. CK BRAY

callisto
publishing
an imprint of Sourcebooks

Published by Callisto Publishing LLC C/O Sourcebooks LLC
P.O. Box 4410, Naperville, Illinois 60567-4410
(630) 961-3900
callistopublishing.com

Library of Congress Cataloging-in-Publication Data

Names: Bray, C. K., 1970-, author.
Title: Your first 90 days managing people : a new manager's guide to
impactful leadership / CK Bray.
Description: Naperville, Illinois : Callisto Publishing LLC 2024. |
Includes bibliographical references and index.
Identifiers: LCCN 2023054404 (print) | LCCN 2023054405 (ebook) | ISBN
9798886509649 (trade paperback) | ISBN 9798886509656 (epub)
Subjects: LCSH: Personnel management. | Leadership.
Classification: LCC HF5549 .B7897 2024 (print) | LCC HF5549 (ebook) | DDC
658.3--dc23/eng/20231222
LC record available at https://lccn.loc.gov/2023054404
LC ebook record available at https://lccn.loc.gov/2023054405

Printed and bound in the United States of America.
VP 10 9 8 7 6 5 4 3 2 1

This book is dedicated to the future leaders who will change the landscape of business and elevate the lives of those they work with by following the simple principles in this book.

CONTENTS

INTRODUCTION

Congratulations! You have been promoted to a management position and have taken the next step in your career. Your hard work and success as an individual contributor have proven you are ready to take on additional responsibilities, help team members develop their career, and ensure your team or department assists with the organization's success.

I am excited to take this leadership journey with you. I clearly remember accepting my first job directly out of university with a *Fortune* 100 organization. I was excited and intimidated by the opportunity, but with a baby on the way, I knew I had to figure out a way to be successful, and success to me meant moving into management as quickly as possible.

As my career progressed and I was promoted, my motives for becoming a leader and manager changed. I quickly learned that a caring and motivating manager could play an influential role in their direct reports' lives. Helping each team member develop new skills and capabilities, and expand their view of what they believed they could accomplish, was worth more than any compensation I received. I won't forget the first time I interviewed potential candidates for a management position and recognized myself in the responses of these incredible applicants. Some candidates focused on climbing the corporate ladder and experiencing continued upward success. In contrast, others recognized the positive impact and influence they could have on others in the organization.

I enjoyed the employee development process so much that I returned to school to earn an MBA and a PhD. I finished my corporate career as the global vice president of organizational development. Shortly thereafter, I started my own company helping large organizations develop, retain, and inspire their employees.

Having experienced the path you are embarking on, both personally and as a consultant, I understand the exciting opportunities before you. I wish you all the best and know you will succeed if you follow the advice, strategies, and tactics you find in this book. The contents contain much more than my advice; they include the advice of more than twenty thousand leaders I have worked with during the course of my career. I have seen their mistakes, their failures, and their successes. By reading this book, you will learn from their experiences and implement their strategies and suggestions. It will help you minimize your shortcomings and expand your strengths. I hope this book helps make your first ninety days some of the most enjoyable of your management career. You will be great.

HOW TO USE THIS BOOK

This book was written as a handbook to guide you during the first three months of your leadership journey. I have included advice, steps, scenarios, and personal examples to illustrate how important each management topic is to your success. I have also included information on specific issues that extend past ninety days and impact the success of your first year as a manager. This book was constructed to be read not only sequentially but also by topic. If you find yourself having an issue, search out the chapter that pertains to your situation and you will find advice on the specific steps to take to move forward.

Each chapter covers a topic I consider essential to understanding your first ninety days as a leader. If you read each chapter and follow the steps, you can avoid common mistakes that new managers make and set yourself apart as a leader who has taken the time to learn and prepare for management.

This book contains the advice of managers and leaders who have been very successful in their careers. I hope the collected wisdom of those who have walked the management path before you is helpful and provides the insights you need to make wise decisions. Remember that leadership is a skill; you will be practicing it for years to come, so give yourself a break when you make a mistake, take what you learned from the experience, and continue to improve. I wish you all the best on your management journey.

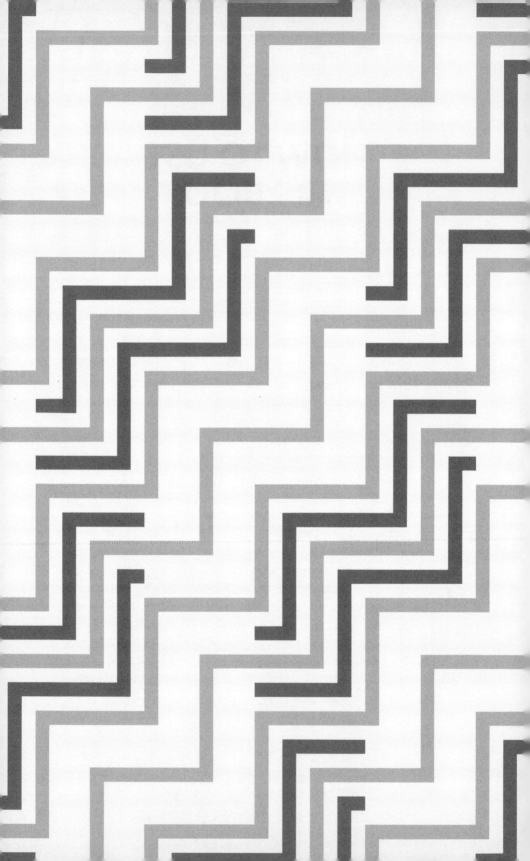

PART I

Learning the Basics of Effective Management

Learning to be an effective manager may initially feel daunting and, at times, overwhelming, but don't fear. The following two chapters will cover the basics of effective, successful, and meaningful management practices. Working together, we will prepare you to successfully navigate the people side of management, work processes, and product results to ensure a successful first ninety days as a new manager. A few of these factors include communication, how to set goals and strategies, training your team, and providing honest and motivating feedback.

Understanding the positive actions first-time managers should take and what common mistakes to avoid will help you manage like a seasoned professional and accelerate your learning as a leader. I wouldn't be an effective mentor if I didn't share the five qualities of a great manager and the tools to implement these qualities from day one to gain the trust and respect of those you lead.

Remember, effective management is a learned skill. You can learn how to be a great leader if you are willing to practice the skills and techniques you learn. Focusing daily on improving will create effective management habits that will last beyond your first ninety days.

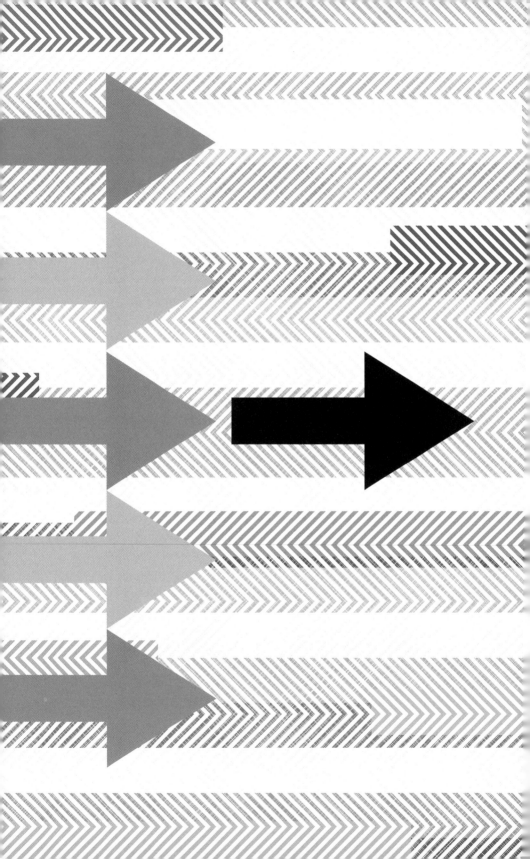

CHAPTER 1

Understanding What It Means to Be a Manager

The role of a manager is fundamental to any organization. Managers are central to ensuring that people and processes are efficient and effective. They facilitate crucial connections between upper management and the workforce. A manager is often the difference between success and failure in an organization. The role of a manager is diverse; there is not one prescribed function they fulfill. A manager's daily responsibilities range from overseeing projects to motivating and inspiring people. The ability to adapt quickly and move from one situation to another is critical. This expansive scope of duties can be difficult, not to mention exhausting, if the right skills and capabilities are not developed.

Managers work with several levels of individuals within an organization. They collaborate with direct reports, counterparts, their boss, and other employees involved in shared projects. They are often the only connection among these individuals and are responsible for creating a single vision that brings all their needs together. In this chapter, we will learn how to manage people, processes, and projects while providing an overview of typical day-to-day managerial responsibilities.

Overcoming a New-Manager Barrier to Success

A successful individual contributor, Sari was an exceptional employee. She always met her yearly goals and objectives, and was willing to provide expertise on projects to new employees. When Sari was promoted to manage an international team, she was determined to work hard and excel as a new manager.

Less than a month into her new position, Sari felt overwhelmed and underqualified. It wasn't only the amount of work that caused these feelings but also the numerous day-to-day responsibilities she experienced. Her six employees were spread throughout the world in different time zones, and each of those employees managed projects Sari had to track to completion. Sari also had an open position, requiring her to lead several weekly interviews. Taking into consideration daily meetings with her manager, client calls, and interactions with other leaders in the organization, Sari felt she was working extremely hard but she wasn't making significant progress on her goals and projects or developing her team.

Sari met with her manager to discuss her current situation and ask for guidance. Remembering feeling the same way, Sari's manager enrolled her in a new-leader course that taught Sari effective management strategies to handle day-to-day responsibilities while still developing and assisting her team. Within weeks Sari noticed a difference as she prioritized and built habits that helped manage her daily tasks while still allowing time to develop her employees.

A Brief Definition of the Manager Role

Amazon currently offers more than sixty thousand books with *leadership* in the title. Yet, even with that number of published books, research has not yet agreed on a definition of leadership other than emphasizing the words *inspiring* and *influencing* others. After twenty-five years of working with organizations in various capacities, I am okay with that definition. However, the nature of leading in today's organizations, whether large or small, encompasses a broader and, in some ways, a grander definition of the manager role.

A manager is someone who not only inspires and influences others but who is also responsible for supervising and motivating employees in their organizational responsibilities. Being a manager means being in the trenches with your team to lead and motivate them in their work. Wow! Having been a manager, I know it can be unexpectedly time-consuming, involved, and at times challenging.

A manager has a monumental task of such importance it requires continuing education throughout their tenure. To assist those you work with to develop their career and skills is a noble and meaningful role. These are the reasons why you need to make the first ninety days matter. Organizations need managers who can take on this demanding role and do it well; it is one of the foundations of organizational success.

The Three Ps of Effective Management

Achieving your goals as a new manager, especially within the first ninety days, requires skills, practice, and the desire to learn and grow from your mistakes. The foundation of your success is built on the three Ps of business: people, processes, and product. Marcus Lemonis, the chair and CEO of Camping World, Good

Sam Enterprises, Gander RV, and The House, refined the idea of the three Ps and the impact people, processes, and products have on individual and organizational success. He provides weekly examples of the three Ps in action on his hit television show, *The Profit*.

The three Ps of business are essential for your success and development. First, every manager must have the best people in the right roles to meet and deliver client and organizational expectations. Second, effective processes need to be in place and routinely followed to ensure consistency and quality, and eliminate mistakes. In addition, having processes in place creates more time for your team to innovate and deliver quality products and services internally and externally.

Finally, ensure your team is delivering the right products and services to meet the needs of the organization and the client. Take time to review "how" and "what" your team delivers to the organization and clients, as this will help increase revenue while retaining current clients and gaining new ones.

THE PEOPLE

People always come first. People are the defining metric in your and the organization's success. Marcus Lemonis teaches managers that "businesses are based on relationships, and relationships are based on people. So, surround yourself with good people." A skilled manager also develops team members. Place people in roles that build on their strengths to bring value to the team and organization. Leverage employees' strengths by providing tasks and projects where they can learn, excel, and lead. To ensure their success, provide training to develop their skills.

Trust your employees within their area of responsibility. Your trust shows your team you value their contributions. Allow them to make decisions and take responsibility for their efforts. When people feel trusted, appreciated, and supported, everyone wins.

THE PROCESS

Hard work, a great product, and good intentions cannot create success without efficient processes and execution of those processes. Therefore, it is essential to have simple, repeatable, scalable, and efficient processes in every work area. Employees want to work efficiently and productively, and processes provide that framework. If people are the organization's lifeblood, processes are the system that carries and sustains that life.

Well-designed processes enhance employees' ability to reach peak performance. Processes increase retention and employee well-being. Processes need to be reassessed and altered frequently based on market, client, and organizational changes. Process analysis should occur often and requires employee feedback and input to reduce inefficiencies.

THE PRODUCT

Once you have the right people and processes in place, the focus moves to your product. It doesn't matter whether you work in a large or small organization or in the technology, healthcare, or service sectors—you provide a product that must bring value to your clients and organization.

The product you deliver reflects your people and processes. As an effective manager, ensure your product meets customer needs and trends. Check in with your customers to identify their needs and ensure your products are well received. Then, look for opportunities to create, modify, or expand your product in this constantly changing business environment.

KNOWING THE INS AND OUTS OF YOUR BUSINESS IS CRUCIAL

On my second day of sailing lessons, I believed I had a strong understanding of how to change my boat's course by adjusting the direction of the mainsail. Unfortunately, what I didn't know was exactly where to sit. When we changed the boat's direction (*tacked*), I was sitting in the wrong place, and the big heavy bar at the foot of the mainsail (the *boom*) swung across the boat and nearly knocked me into the water. I had a gap in my knowledge that almost cost me my head. A knowledge gap may jeopardize your business or put your career at risk.

A few critical areas to have deep knowledge and understanding of include:

▸ Business processes

▸ Customers

▸ Employees

▸ Financial information (the numbers!)

▸ Products

▸ Where vital information and documents are stored

Managers often focus on the current successes and problems of a business and neglect learning about and understanding critical areas that affect the success of their teams and businesses. As with the sailing example, a problem may be heading your way if you do not have sufficient knowledge of vital aspects of your business and team members. And that issue may come as an unwelcome surprise if you're not careful.

Spending a little time each week learning and reviewing key aspects of your business will help you avoid pitfalls and make better business decisions.

Typical Day-to-Day Managerial Responsibilities

At the end of a performance review with an exceptional employee, the individual tentatively asked if I would answer an odd question that might hurt my feelings. I was intrigued.

"I promise I will not be offended," I assured her. "Go ahead and ask."

"What do you do all day?" she asked.

I laughed and responded, "I don't know—a bit of everything!"

I promised to compile a list over the next month to share with her, and we would both find out the answer to her question. The following list has changed over the years and is certainly not exhaustive. I realize that certain responsibilities are more relevant to specific industries and market sectors than others.

Typical day-to-day managerial responsibilities include a wide range of activities. One is communicating information to several levels of an organization. Another is attending meetings— a *lot* of meetings. During these meetings, goals and projects are discussed, and managers create and implement strategies related to organizational goals. Finally, one of the most important daily responsibilities is hiring, training, and developing employees. Managers also provide feedback and, if needed, terminate employment.

One daily responsibility that surprises new managers is the time spent responding to emails and messaging platforms such as Slack or Microsoft Teams. According to several studies, managers may spend up to 40 percent of their day checking email and instant messages. This is nearly three or four hours a day and continues to increase as communication becomes increasingly virtual. Moreover, managers often have their own projects and assignments in addition to these responsibilities.

COMMUNICATING INFORMATION

Communication within a team impacts productivity, culture, and the relationship between managers and employees. Communicating often with employees has been shown to have short- and long-term benefits for the team and the organization.

Choosing how you communicate with your team is as important as the message. Matching the method of communication with the information can detract from or enhance how the message is received. Think about the type of information you are delivering and what the best method of delivery would be: email, Zoom meeting, instant message, or phone call? For example, providing feedback should always be done in person or via phone, where an individual can ask questions and discuss solutions, versus an instant message, which is a one-way communication.

SETTING MEETINGS AND GOALS

The brain loves goals. When you set a goal, the neurotransmitter dopamine is released, and you are motivated to action. Dopamine also spikes when you are close to reaching your goal. Goals are the vehicle to peak performance. Without clear markers of achievement, employees get sidetracked or misunderstand expectations, causing barriers to success.

An effective manager motivates employees to achieve more through goal setting, holds them accountable, and praises achievement. Research has found that setting goals increases employees' connections with their team and organization. It is important to remember that every outstanding achievement occurred because the individual had a goal.

Goal setting is also imperative for providing ongoing developmental feedback. When you establish specific goals and objectives, you can provide weekly and monthly feedback on performance, track progress, celebrate successes, and motivate through difficult situations and barriers.

CREATING AND IMPLEMENTING STRATEGIES

As a new leader, you don't usually create organizational strategies but instead implement them. It is typically up to managers to execute strategies successfully. Strategy implementation requires you to delegate the work to the team, provide a timeline of execution, and monitor the team's progress and performance while providing support and motivation.

TRAINING

One of the most rewarding aspects of managing others is watching an individual's skills, capabilities, and performance develop. When you spend time and resources on training, you provide more than job upskilling and development; you give them an opportunity for career advancement, pay increases, and a change in their mindset and belief about what they can achieve.

Research has shown when you train and develop your team, productivity, engagement, and retention increase. In addition, trained employees are happier, feel increased self-worth in their role, and have higher morale. Be known for helping employees build a career and develop their talents and skills. I have fond memories of my first manager, an expert in helping those he managed to succeed in their current role and preparing them for their next role or promotion.

MONITORING PROGRESS AND DELIVERABLES

For a project to stay on track and a strategy to be executed correctly, employees and teams must remain focused on meeting their objectives. This requires a timeline of when each deliverable is due and who is responsible for that deliverable. An effective manager checks in regularly on the team's progress, solves problems, and encourages and motivates the team. A good manager also helps when a project stalls or a deadline is fast approaching. This responsibility requires attention to detail; apps and platforms for managers can help make this responsibility easier.

PROVIDING EVALUATION AND FEEDBACK

In the fast-paced, ever-changing virtual work environment, feedback and manager evaluation play a critical role in talent development, problem-solving, morale improvement, and motivating individuals and teams. Effective managers enjoy providing positive feedback and praise about their employees' work; however, sharing developmental or negative feedback can be difficult for both the manager and the receiver. To overcome this difficulty, effective managers should share positive and developmental feedback often (at least once a week) and quickly (three to five minutes). Creating a trusting environment of open dialogue requires frequent feedback that is not overwhelming. Think of these as short bursts of feedback and motivation.

HIRING OR TERMINATING EMPLOYEES

Effective management is filled with highs and lows. It is exciting to interview and hire an individual to join your team. The hiring experience cultivates a manager/employee relationship different from any other workplace association. Learning to effectively interview, ask questions, decipher a candidate's skills and competencies, and onboard your new team member is of paramount importance for a manager when they are building a high-performing team. Hiring excellent employees is a solid signal to senior leadership of an effective manager.

Terminating employees is considered one of the manager's most challenging responsibilities. Ensure you know your company's process for terminating an employee. Communicate often with human resources and avoid going through this process alone. Seek the assistance of senior managers who can help you navigate this new experience.

BE PREPARED FOR YOUR RESPONSIBILITIES TO EVOLVE

Every recent business article I have read mentions the Volatile, Uncertain, Complex, and Ambiguous (VUCA) world of work. We live in a world where we are increasingly connecting in new ways, with automation, technology, and Zoom (to name only a few) changing how business is conducted. Based on these changes, there is an emerging need for employee skills that enable adaptive responses to quick, unfamiliar changes. Your success as a manager this year and into the future will heavily depend on your ability to change and evolve while also managing change for your team.

Change will continue to occur due to increased global connection and technological advances such as workplace tools, software, and other programs. Often these are introduced to eliminate, scale down, or increase ease of work, but they cause cognitive overload and increase work time by causing a shift in long-standing processes.

The COVID-19 pandemic and its aftermath are excellent examples of how managers must evolve. For example, team management changed from working together in an office to holding Zoom meetings while working from home. Although this shift felt drastic at the time, researchers are predicting other large-scale changes to the workplace in technology, automation, and ongoing work/lifestyle changes in the coming years.

Be prepared for your job responsibilities, clients, and "ways of working" to evolve and change. Choosing to be adaptable in embracing change, learning new skills, and navigating new processes will contribute to your success as a manager.

Learning to Manage Takes Time

I was on a lunch break during a company meeting, and one of my favorite leaders sat next to me. He was the epitome of an incredible manager. His team performed well year after year, and he had the ability to discover people with incredible talent and develop them for his leadership team. During our discussion, I asked him for suggestions on steps I could take to become a great leader. His response was: "Time!" This wasn't the answer I was expecting, but he explained that becoming great at anything requires time, hard work, and effort.

He shared that as a new employee in the organization, he focused on helping other team members be successful. As a result, he was quickly promoted to district manager based on his achievements and competence as a salesperson. However, two months into his new role, he couldn't believe how hard it was to get the organization and other leaders to change and innovate. He was worried he was on the road to failure and felt stressed most of the time. He credited this time as a period of forging and discovering his management philosophies and leadership style by making good and bad decisions.

"Managing is a learning process and takes time, so allow yourself time to develop into a great manager," he said. "Choose one area to develop and work on that area until you master it, then move on to another." Looking back, he was right—go easy on yourself and allow yourself time to learn how to manage.

Key Takeaways

Learning the basics of effective management is the first step on your leadership journey. Understanding how people, processes, and products (the three Ps) impact your day-to-day responsibilities prepares you for your role as a new manager. Reread the key takeaways at least once a month to remind yourself what is important.

→ The foundation of effective management is built on the three Ps of business: people, processes, and product.

→ Effective managers are involved in various daily activities, from attending meetings and setting goals to creating and implementing strategies. Motivating, training, monitoring progress, and providing feedback to your employees are critical functions of your role.

→ Learn the skill of interviewing, asking questions, deciphering a candidate's skills, and onboarding your new team members. Hiring competent, high-performing individuals is a signal to senior leadership of an effective manager.

→ Constant and consistent change will continue to affect you and your organization. Due to technology, new workplace tools, and software, be prepared to evolve as your job responsibilities, clients, and "ways of working" shift. Be adaptable by embracing change, learning new skills, and navigating new processes.

→ It takes time to learn how to manage. Focus on the three Ps and realize you will make mistakes and learn from them.

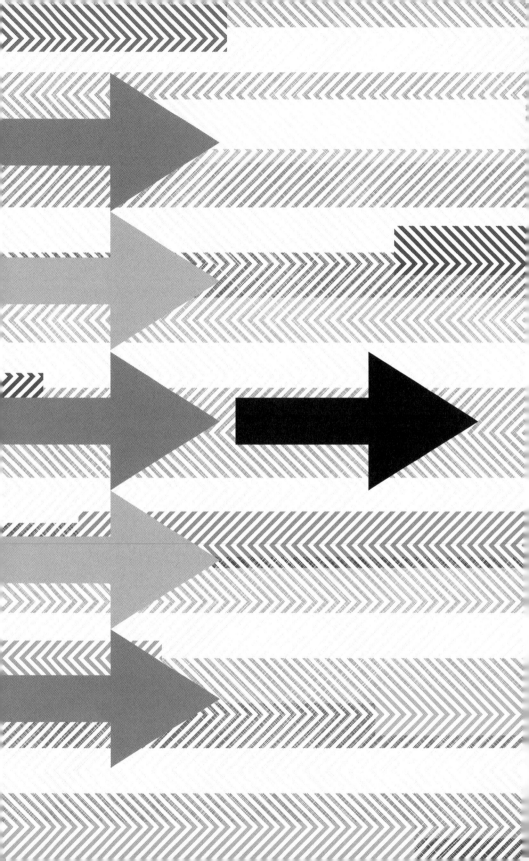

CHAPTER **2**

The Dos and Don'ts of First-Time Managers

When I accepted my first corporate role directly out of college, my new manager invited me to an expensive restaurant to celebrate my joining the sales team. As we sat at the table, I noticed more than nine different utensils surrounding the plate on either side and three at the top. (To clear my mother's name, she had taught me which utensils to use at a nice dinner, but I quickly realized she had neglected to mention six others.) My new manager noticed my panic and said, "I will teach you the dos and don'ts of using the right utensils. Follow my lead and always start with the utensils on the outside and work in."

As you begin this journey as a new manager, I offer the same advice my first manager provided: I will teach you the dos and don'ts of first-time managers. This chapter will help you avoid common pitfalls new managers make and spotlight areas and behaviors research has shown to create great managers. In addition, I will cover the five qualities of a good manager, the common mistakes new managers make, and how a mentor can help you navigate your first ninety days. You will be well on your way to starting strong if you carefully read and implement what you learn.

Motivating Disengaged Employees

While walking out to catch the train after an end-of-day Friday meeting, Dion was stunned and hurt to overhear two of his direct reports' conversations. "I feel so alive when I walk out of the office on a Friday afternoon; I can't help but raise my arms like I'm finishing a marathon." Dion's other direct report added, "An uphill-both-ways marathon!" Dion was still thinking about that conversation when he met with his manager on Monday. "They always comment negatively about the workplace, and I'm doing everything possible to make it a positive environment since we returned to the office."

Instead of reassuring Dion that it wasn't his fault, his manager shared the latest research on employee satisfaction: "The Gallup State of the Global Workplace study was recently released, and it found 51 percent of employees were actively searching or watching for job opportunities. However, another Gallup study found that 85 percent of employees worldwide are disengaged and don't like their jobs."

Wanting Dion to look at the direct reports' conversation from a new perspective, his manager posed two questions: "What things do you need to *start* doing to be a great manager?" and "What things do you need to *stop* doing to be a great manager?" I pose the same questions to you throughout this chapter.

The 5 Qualities of a Good Manager

"She was the best boss to work for; I would have followed her wherever she went!" I often heard statements like this while interviewing more than 1,500 corporate workers for a leadership-development course. Still, I wondered what "being a great manager" meant and what it looked like on a typical workday. What activities, behaviors, and communication set apart the great boss from the mediocre one?

I found the answer in one of my PhD behavioral psychology classes. Great managers have qualities that transition their employee's brains to a reward state. Your brain codes every situation, encounter, and experience as a threat or a reward. Great managers communicate, listen, demonstrate confidence, and support their team members and direct reports in a way that is perceived as a reward. The manager is viewed as someone to train, develop, and help them succeed, even if it means having difficult conversations. The key to the five qualities of a good manager is not only exhibiting them but also understanding what quality your direct report needs at a specific time.

STRONG COMMUNICATION

Studies show managers spend as much as 80 percent of the workday communicating. Skilled managers understand that the success of their team relies on clear communication. Effective managers talk, listen, present, and share information clearly with their employees. A strong communicator conveys information thoroughly and is receptive to other employees' feedback. In practice, managers relay easily understood instructions so everyone is on the same page and the chance for confusion is minimized. In addition, managers are more effective at managing teams and getting desired results if they communicate often and clearly.

ACTIVE LISTENING SKILLS

People respond positively to individuals who listen to them. Listening is a crucial attribute of a good manager, yet few managers have mastered this skill. One of the main complaints about managers is their lack of attention and listening during meetings and conversations.

Active listening skills are demonstrated by engaging with a person and connecting with what they are saying. This can be exhibited by responding "Yes" or "I understand," or asking pertinent and applicable questions. Active listening is restating what you hear the individual say to ensure understanding and comprehension. Likewise, active listening requires focused attention and eye contact. These nonverbal cues help the speaker, or the employee, feel their words are heard. Employees are validated by active listening and feeling seen, heard, and understood. For a manager, active listening builds trust between employees, increases comprehension of the situation, and broadens understanding of the business. It is essential to listen, and then listen more.

DEMONSTRATE CONFIDENCE

Individuals follow those they believe will help them succeed. Demonstrating confidence in the workplace is exhibiting a strong belief in your ability to succeed in your leadership. Confident managers know their skills and expertise, and use them to benefit the company. According to research, four ways to increase confidence are maintaining a confident posture, making direct eye contact, remaining composed, and retaining a professional appearance. In addition, it is vital to appear confident and provide employees with a sense of security. Employees who trust their manager have found to be more productive.

SUPPORTING TEAM MEMBERS AND DIRECT REPORTS

Supporting team members as a manager incorporates playing an active and encouraging role in the employees' work. Team members know when they are supported by their manager's frequent messages and praise. Keeping up with employees over the long term demonstrates the manager cares about their improvement; invested managers increase motivation.

This support is best demonstrated by frequent one-on-one meetings. In one-on-one meetings, effective managers open dialogue on projects and discuss roadblocks their employees encounter. Motivating direct reports produces the maximum output of their abilities and fosters a collaborative and supportive workplace.

ABILITY TO MANAGE THROUGH CHANGE

The ability of a manager to navigate uncertainty and change while keeping the team focused on productivity and performance is a complex responsibility that has recently emerged as a necessity for managers. It is a difficult skill to master, because the brain dislikes uncertainty. As managers, we like to provide answers and solutions to problems. However, constant change robs managers of the ability to provide certainty and solutions. Along with change come uneasy feelings and negative thoughts about possible outcomes. These negative thoughts are a normal human tendency, but they can become roadblocks to job performance, potential, and professional fulfillment if not controlled or diverted.

When a change occurs, help your team accept and embrace the change. For example, if a new computer system is rolled out, encourage your team to be the first to embrace the change and become experts in the new system so they can assist others. This moves the employees' perception from uncertainty and negativity to be motivated to accept and learn the new computer process. This method works for all changes experienced in a work environment. First, help direct reports accept and embrace the change. Then motivate them to find a reason to change.

HAVING A MENTOR WILL MAKE YOU AN EVEN BETTER MANAGER

Taking the step from individual contributor to a managerial role is a big transition requiring new leadership skills. The role of a new manager can be overwhelming and lonely. Seek a trusted mentor with whom you can have a confidential conversation and who will provide new perspectives, insights, and valuable knowledge as you navigate the first year of management. Mentors can help you avoid common pitfalls by sharing their experiences and providing feedback and guidance on decisions, problems you encounter, and ways you can improve.

Having a mentor has extensive benefits, including:

► Exposure to new perspectives, ideas, and approaches to problems and barriers

► Improved job proficiency

► Increased likelihood of achieving goals

► Increased sense of belonging

► Increased sense of well-being, confidence at work, and belief in one's capabilities

► Positive business outcomes

Common Mistakes New Managers Make

When I walked into the training room on my first day of new management training, a slide was up on the screen that read:

1 out of 10 managers has the natural skills to be a great leader.

I sat down and wondered how bad the other new managers must feel, knowing they had a lot to learn.

Unfortunately, a Gallup research study found that most managers (myself included) didn't know they were failing and making mistakes that hurt their team's performance, collaboration, and ability to overcome obstacles. To help you avoid these pitfalls and navigate your first ninety days as a manager, the most common mistakes new managers make are: not setting clear goals, micromanaging direct reports, being unreceptive to feedback, and trying to be "friends" or maintain prior relationships with direct reports. These pitfalls can hinder your development.

NOT SETTING CLEAR GOALS

Everyone talks about the benefits of setting goals and the positive outcomes that can occur, but rarely is it discussed what will happen if you don't set goals. Let's look at the other side of the goal coin. If you don't have goals and don't think about what you want to accomplish in your future, then you are thirty times more likely not to have them occur *and* to forgo the benefits of what achieving those goals will bring. Knowing the consequences of not setting goals, one would think everyone would be setting them, but only 14 percent of people set goals for themselves. Be wise and set clear goals.

MICROMANAGING

Micromanaging is a management style in which the manager overly controls the minute details of an employee's work. Micro-managers resist delegating work, are excessively involved in their employees' efforts, and ask for frequent updates. A joint study by Harvard Business School professor Teresa Amabile and psychologist Steven Kramer showed that micromanagement "stifles creativity and productivity in the long run." Adverse effects of micromanaging range from increased stress and burnout to decreased productivity. Employees who are micromanaged reported decreased job satisfaction and increased distrust of their leader, and they were more likely to leave the organization due to the manager.

BEING UNRECEPTIVE TO FEEDBACK

Feedback must be a two-way street between a manager and their direct reports. When a manager is unreceptive to feedback, it harms the working relationship. This occurs when a manager becomes overly defensive when presented with constructive criticism. In the moment, ineffective managers negate what is being said, do not make eye contact, or respond with hostility. Instead, great leaders listen openly and respond to the criticism, even if they disagree with the feedback.

When receiving feedback, poor managers may choose to ignore the comments and not reflect on what is shared with them. They may also discredit the information. One negative consequence of being unreceptive to feedback is that employees lose trust and respect for managers. Employees may also be less likely to receive feedback and react similarly to the manager.

BEING TOO FRIENDLY OR SEEKING TO BE LIKED

Two months into her role as a new manager, Sarah felt lonely in her new management position. The friendships and camaraderie she had felt with her former colleagues had changed since she was promoted. She didn't receive as many phone calls, was out of the loop on the office gossip, and didn't get invited to lunch or after-work functions. "I didn't change as a person; I only took on a different role," she thought. This feeling caused Sarah to be overly friendly with her direct reports and treat them as friends, trying to maintain a friendship similar to what they shared before her promotion.

Although it is essential to be genuine, kind, and open, new managers must learn that relationships change as individuals take on new organizational roles. Therefore, a manager must maintain a certain level of professionalism and maintain a manager/direct report relationship. Remember, you will provide direct reports with their yearly reviews, decide salary increases and bonuses, and recommend them for promotions. Being too friendly may appear to influence your decisions.

THE IMPACT OF POOR MANAGEMENT ON PRODUCTIVITY

Managers are vital to the success of their people and the processes; poor management can be the downfall of a team. Unfortunately, almost everyone has a "bad manager" story from their work history. They are stories we never forget. For example, a manager asked me why I expensed an ice cream cone on a Sunday evening. When I explained that I was driving Sunday evening because I had an early client meeting in another part of the state and wanted to be sure to get in a full day's work, she told me, "It looks bad." So, I never scheduled an early morning meeting again; instead, I would leave on Monday morning and spend most of the day driving, not with clients.

How detrimental can poor management be to an organization? Research has shown it can drastically decrease the efficiency with which a company produces goods and services and reduce profits. I was a perfect example of this. This decrease happens in two ways; first, poor management creates low employee morale. When processes are inefficient, people become frustrated and lack direction. When employee performance decreases, productivity inevitably goes down.

Second, poor management has a ripple effect; processes suffer, profits decline, and people become discouraged and lose interest in their work. People thrive when they see success. Also, employees who don't feel cared for are less likely to go the extra mile in their work. Good managers are the backbone of any organization and carry a heavy weight.

Lead with an Open Hand, Not an Iron Fist

Managers have taken on new responsibilities in the past few years. Their focus on performance has been split with other demanding employee needs such as taking care of their own health; working from home; dealing with the grief, loneliness, and loss associated with the pandemic; and experiencing increased stress and anxiety levels. All these factors have caused a significant decrease in employees' mental and physical health.

Empathy and *compassion* are often used interchangeably, but they have different meanings. Compassion seeks to understand and respond to what another individual is feeling and then be open to finding ways to alleviate their suffering. Compassion is feeling *for* others and having a willingness to act. On the other hand, empathy is understanding the other person's experience; it is feeling *with* the person. It is experiencing many of the same emotions as they are. Moving from empathy to compassion and vulnerability changes the culture of a team and organization.

Studies have shown organizations that focus on compassion, empathy, and vulnerability have employees with reduced stress and more job satisfaction. In addition, workplace compassion and vulnerability also cause an increase in loyalty, employee retention, dedication, and employee engagement, to name only a few.

Compassionate and vulnerable managers are open to learning and have a growth mindset. They welcome feedback and are driven to improve their skills. Compassionate and vulnerable leaders are easily approachable. They are solutions-focused and seek to understand the causes of failure or underachieving. They seek to influence and inspire rather than provide orders.

Key Takeaways

As you begin your management journey, learn from managers who have come before you: It is like having a crystal ball that provides you with information to succeed in the future. Reread these key takeaways at least once a month to remind yourself of these first-time managers' dos and don'ts:

→ The five qualities of a good manager are strong communication, active listening skills, demonstrating confidence, supporting team members and direct reports, and the ability to manage through change and uncertainty.

→ Having a trustworthy mentor, especially during the first year of being a manager, helps you navigate toward the five qualities each manager should possess.

→ Avoid the common mistakes new managers make, including not setting clear goals with their team members, micromanaging, and wanting work done "their" way. Other common mistakes include being unreceptive to feedback or being too "friendly" in the hope that their team will like them.

→ There is a difference between being buddy-buddy and leading with compassion, care, and vulnerability. It is crucial to humanize leadership by showing who you are as an individual.

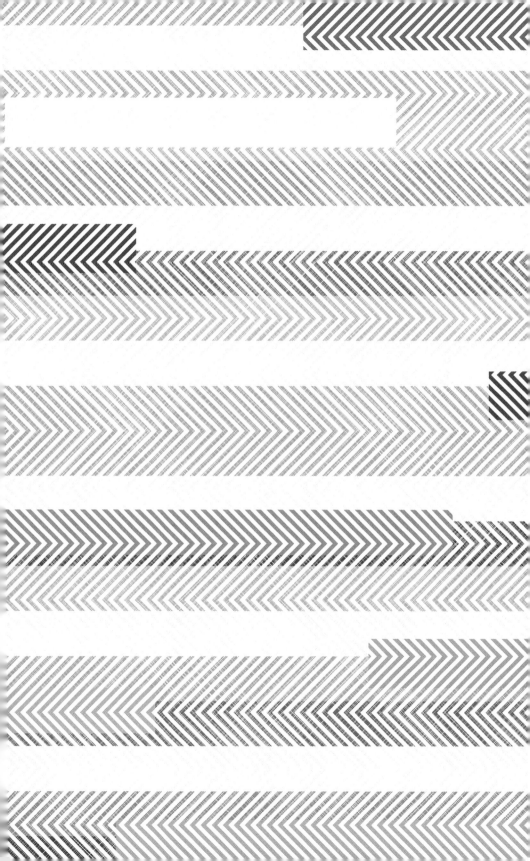

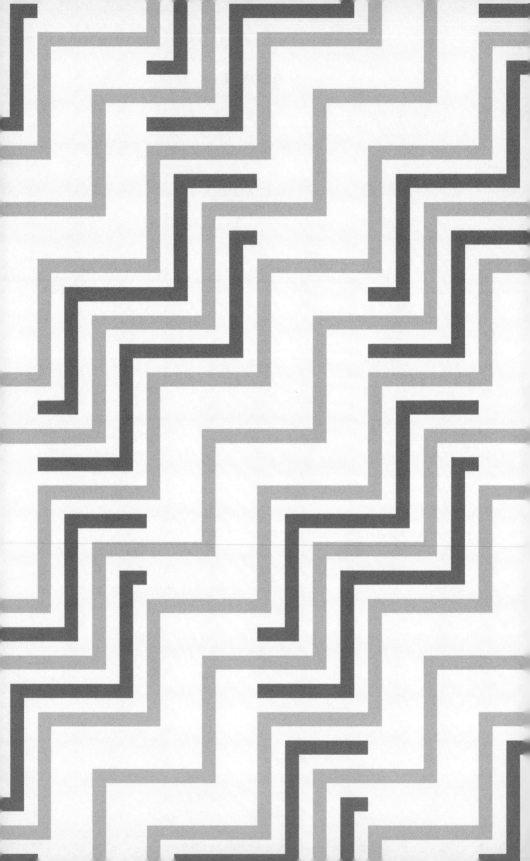

PART II

Your First 30 Days
Building a Strong Foundation with Your Colleagues

"It is crucial to always start strong; it sets the tone for the rest of the match," my high school tennis coach would say before every tournament. The same advice applies to your position as a new manager. Developing the right managerial habits, relationships, and behaviors from the beginning sets a tone for who you are and how you work as a leader. In addition, creating early wins in your first thirty days will build credibility and momentum that will immediately impact your people, colleagues, and projects.

This section is designed to provide you with approaches that create immediate impact in a short period. Focusing on these areas will help build a strong foundation with your colleagues.

I provide specific steps and examples for each topic, ranging from implementing the five strategies of creating rapport and fostering trust to identifying why employees might distrust their manager. Also, defining your management style and sharing it with others will be crucial to your success.

Focusing daily on minor improvements will help your first thirty days be a success and launch your managerial career in a positive direction.

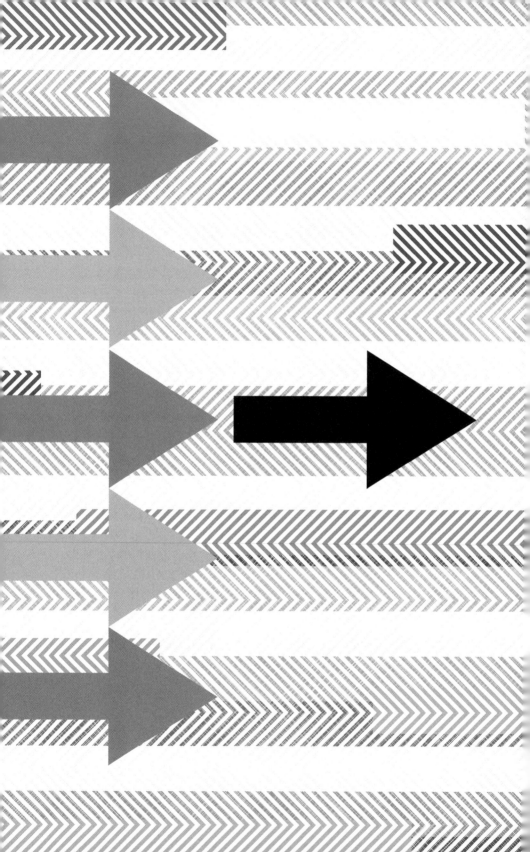

CHAPTER **3**

Fostering Trust with Your Direct Reports

Trust is the beginning of every strong workplace relationship. Your initial discussions with your direct reports are vital to building a relationship and your success (and happiness!) as a manager. Your direct reports want you to trust them, and they want to trust you. Trust can be one of the most effective forms of motivation.

After a promotion, managers are often enrolled in leadership-development classes to develop their abilities in coaching, communication, conflict resolution, and employee motivation, to name a few. These elements all have an effect on productivity and employee engagement, but recent research has shown one surprising characteristic proves to be a superhero trait—the ability to build rapport and trust with your direct reports.

Google's famous research on teams studied 180 teams and discovered the best predictor of achievement and performance was a culture of trust. Key strategies for creating meaningful rapport and deep trust with your direct reports include being authentic, keeping your word, praising others in public and criticizing in private, creating attainable challenges, and providing autonomy. Each strategy influences different aspects of trust, which we will discuss in detail.

This Is Exactly What *They* Need

Early in my consulting career, my colleagues and I at the Adaption Institute were working with a division of a multinational organization. The topic of the leadership-development course we facilitated was dealing with conflict in a way that builds trust and strengthens relationships. During lunch on the first day, one of the leaders said, "This is such great content! We have learned a lot, but our client-facing counterparts are the individuals and team who need this information."

A few months later, we facilitated the same content for the client-facing team. Like clockwork, one of the participants approached me at lunch and said, "This information is incredible, and it will help us, but you know who *really* needs this? Our leadership team." I quickly realized that the problem with building trust was blamed on others and outward-focused rather than internally focused at this organization.

As a new manager, it doesn't matter if every process isn't what it should be or if your organization's culture isn't built on trust. What matters is you! You have the power to create trust within your team and with your direct reports. Trust begins with you and every interaction you have, each decision you make, and the coaching you provide. You can enhance trust and build relationships by taking ownership of yourself, your department, and your team. It is never exactly what *they* need. But it is exactly what *you* need.

Why Trust Is Vital to Successful Working Relationships

We have been told trust always goes both ways, but research on trust in the workplace shows a different story. According to the Edelman Trust Barometer—a yearly annual trust and credibility survey of 33,000 people in twenty-eight countries—one in three employees doesn't trust their employer. To make matters worse, trust decreases from the top of the organization down to frontline employees. It was found that 64 percent of executives trust their organization while only 48 percent of employees do. Unfortunately, employees trust their peers more than those at the top of the corporate ladder.

The level of distrust has been at a record high since the pandemic and the increase in employees virtually working. But trust in the workplace is vital to both individual and team success. Trust among a team builds communication, and communication is how work gets done. Trust also increases productivity and motivation. When employees feel a manager or counterpart trusts them, they are more likely to work harder so that they don't let their manager down. Trust also improves employee satisfaction. Research published in the *Harvard Business Review* found that employees in a high-trust workplace are more satisfied than employees in a low-trust environment. Trust is a compelling influencer of employee productivity, happiness, and job satisfaction. This directly translates to the organization's success; if employees are productive and happy, organizational performance improves.

Build Trust by Getting to Know Your Company's Culture

Jane had finally landed her dream job. She was coaching executives, and, as a freelance contractor, she could set her hours and work from home. The organization that hired Jane appeared organized, friendly, supportive, and focused on performance and client satisfaction to her during the interview process. Fast-forward three months, and Jane had lost all trust in the organization. They were disorganized, did not follow through on promises made when Jane was hired, and mistreated employees. They kept reassuring Jane that they were in a "period of growth and transition, and things would not be hectic forever." As Jane began looking for a new job, she knew she was experiencing the actual company culture, and things would not change but most likely only deteriorate.

A company's culture isn't developed overnight, and it doesn't change quickly. However, culture is always evolving. Culture is deeply rooted in the company's past and the leadership that guides the organization. Culture is stronger than yearly goals or strategies because it is unspoken and based on assumptions, perceptions, group norms, and thoughts on how an individual can succeed and progress within an organization. I believe the business slogan often attributed to Peter Drucker: "Culture eats strategy for breakfast."

Culture and leadership are woven together. For that reason, understanding your company's culture is essential to building trust; knowing the unspoken norms, rules, and ways of behavior guides a manager in building trust. For example, some cultures create collaborative work environments where individuals help and support one another. Others may be more focused on performance and the attainment of goals. Understanding the culture allows the manager to build trust.

Common Reasons Why Employees Might Distrust Their Manager

Jane experienced every reason employees don't trust their managers or organizations. Yet, in the workplace, trust between employees and managers is the foundation upon which success is built. One of the critical responsibilities of a manager is to foster the trust of their employees. In "The Neuroscience of Trust," an article in the January 2017 *Harvard Business Review*, Paul Zak wrote that compared with people at low-trust companies, people at high-trust companies report:

→ 74 percent less stress

→ 106 percent more energy at work

→ 50 percent higher productivity

→ 13 percent fewer sick days

→ 76 percent more engagement

→ 29 percent more satisfaction with their lives

→ 40 percent less burnout

Trust is a critical factor for personal, team, and organization success. Because of the negative impact of distrust of a manager, good managers should strive to build trust with their employees by being authentic and keeping promises.

Common failings that typically result in a loss of trust are ambiguity, arrogance, and inconsistency between words and actions. Employee turnover increases significantly when employees feel their boss is untrustworthy or dishonest. Those who choose to stay are less productive, less driven, and more cynical about the instruction a manager provides. An effective leader aims to create a work environment where everyone is heard and appreciated.

LACK OF REGULAR COMMUNICATION OR FACE TIME

As a result of the COVID-19 pandemic, many workers who previously worked in an office setting are working from home instead. This change has had a negative effect on communication between managers and employees. Employees who rarely experience face-to-face contact with their manager or regular virtual communication feel disconnected from their leaders. Without regular communication, misunderstandings are more common. Research has found that if employees see and communicate with their managers regularly, they view them as responsible and dependable and feel a stronger workplace relationship.

DISORGANIZED, DISHONEST, OR OPAQUE COMMUNICATION

Disorganized and opaque communication mean the manager does not convey instructions, expectations, feedback, or requirements in an understandable fashion. In turn, employees are unable to work efficiently or effectively. When managers lack the ability to communicate clearly, employees may view them as incompetent. Dishonesty from a manager can be even more insidious. There may be times as a manager when you are required to hold back information, but manipulating information will create problems. Unethical conduct or communication can cause an immediate loss of trust between employees and managers. Remember, employees usually know when they are experiencing dishonest or opaque communication. Without trust, it is difficult for managers to motivate employees.

UNFAIR OR UNEQUAL TREATMENT

One top motivator for employees is fairness. Employees who feel they are treated fairly perform better, help their co-workers, and are less likely to quit. When employees feel they have been mistreated or received unequal treatment, it creates a hostile environment among co-workers and destroys collaboration and team contribution. Likewise, unjustly treated employees often attribute this poor behavior to their manager's inability to be an effective leader. Effective leaders create an equal workplace where employees feel safe and valued.

INEFFECTIVE LEADERSHIP

Ineffective leadership causes employees to distrust their leaders and produce subpar work. Two effects of poor leadership in the workplace are lack of engagement/motivation and high employee turnover. Increased engagement and motivation stem from strong direction and a clear path to achieving desired outcomes. Without a strong leader who sets goals, morale lowers and employees struggle to succeed. When employees feel unguided and unsupported, they often transition to different teams or companies that focus on their development.

ARROGANCE

Arrogant managers are often the most toxic managers in a workplace. A narcissistic boss is highly unlikely to listen to the needs and views of others. Instead, they take credit for other individuals' work and focus on their success and progression. Employees of arrogant leaders are less inclined to work hard because they feel underappreciated and unseen. In turn, their employees do not trust their boss to provide them with feedback that will be helpful for their success.

DEFINING YOUR PERSONAL MANAGEMENT STYLE

My co-worker Steven was driven and relentless while building his career. He read every book about top business people, from Steve Jobs to Elon Musk to Indra Nooyi, and wanted to emulate them. Quite often, in conversations, he would discuss all the exceptional qualities of these individuals. He was anxious to follow in their footsteps and wanted opportunities to lead and influence others. The problem was that he struggled as soon as he was promoted to manager. He was so busy imitating other leaders that he came across as inauthentic and insincere. He didn't take time to figure out his personal management style based on *his* strengths.

When building and defining your personal management style, rule number one is to be yourself. *You* were promoted to be the manager, not Elon Musk. Be confident in your leadership ability and stop looking to others to create your management style. Look at your strengths: What are you good at? Why have you been successful in the past? Decide how you will communicate, provide feedback, and motivate your team members. You need to know who you will be as a leader and be sure you fill this role with *you*, not someone you read about in a book.

Second, capitalize on your strengths. Every manager has unique strengths and development areas. Know who you are and what you bring to the table. Take time to reflect on how you can be the best manager based on your strengths and abilities.

How to Manage Your Former Peers

When you are promoted and become a manager, it is an exciting time and one that is also full of worry and stress. If you have been promoted to managing individuals who were once your peers, this can be a tricky transition. You want to establish yourself as a credible leader and motivate your former peers to high performance while maintaining workplace relationships. There are three steps to making a smooth transition from peer to manager.

First, don't make any drastic changes immediately. You need to lead the team without damaging those peer relationships. It is like walking a tightrope; at the beginning, you are the manager and still a peer. So, make a few small decisions initially, but wait to make more significant decisions until you have been in the role for a more extended period.

Second, establish your credibility early by acting on clarifying your vision and goals, and leading the group. This establishes your personal management style while also sharing what you are thinking about and how you plan to improve the department and team.

Third, as difficult as this will be, you must create some distance from your former peers. Once you have been promoted to manager, the peer-to-peer relationship you shared will change. This is a normal transition required for you to coach, provide feedback, and oversee projects and performance.

As a relatively new employee, I was disappointed when the manager who hired me was promoted. We had an excellent relationship, and I enjoyed working for him. I always thought I was one of his favorites but, after he left, I learned everyone felt the same way. When his replacement was announced, I was worried about what would change, what type of manager the individual would be, and if we would get along. During our first team meeting, he let us know we would each have an hour-long one-on-one with him to discuss our current projects and expectations and get to know each other better. I looked forward to the meeting and sharing what I was working on and had accomplished since joining the organization. Unfortunately, three months passed, and we never talked for more than fifteen minutes. All my information about him came from short meetings, discussions with counterparts, and hearsay from other employees. Some of the information was positive and some was negative. I felt like I was working with a stranger.

Your first thirty days must include a one-on-one with each direct report. It is an opportunity for you to get to know your team members and learn about their current projects, past successes, and expectations for the future. It is an opportunity for your direct report to get personal with you and for you to get personal with them. It opens the lines of communication and begins to build trust. Be sure to continue one-on-ones monthly so you can check in on development, improve performance, and continue to build trust.

5 Strategies for Creating a Rapport with Your Team

Developing your team members is crucial to your success and the organization's success; that's why you must build a strong relationship with each of your team members. Strong rapport with your direct reports helps you navigate complex projects and quick timelines. As you build rapport through being authentic, keeping your word, praising in public and criticizing in private, creating attainable challenges, and providing autonomy, you build a relationship of trust that will be beneficial during difficult times. Let's dive deeper into each of these strategies.

BE AUTHENTIC

I was taught a valuable lesson on authenticity in an exit interview I conducted with an employee. Speaking of her manager, the employee shared, "I don't believe I ever met the real Natalie; she always had on her boss mask. I never got to know or see her in a way I could trust her."

To be authentic managers, leaders need to exhibit self-awareness and genuineness. In "How To Become a Better Leader," published in the MIT *Sloan Management Review*, the authors cited self-awareness as the most important characteristic for leaders to develop. A strategy for developing self-awareness is understanding yourself, your emotions, and your weaknesses. Authentic managers are open about their strengths and weaknesses. To be genuine, ask for suggestions and help from your team. Write them down to show you listened and want to implement their ideas.

KEEP YOUR WORD

The fastest way to build rapport and trust is to keep your word. Breaking your word is also the quickest way to destroy a relationship and trust. Keeping your word is a thread that runs through the other five strategies because it is the foundation of a trusting relationship. Follow this pattern in building rapport and trust with a new team member:

1. Find a need with your direct report and make a commitment to them. Be sure to follow through. Then do it again.

2. When making a promise or commitment, be sure it is realistic and has a completion time. Be careful not to overpromise and underdeliver.

3. If you miscalculate a commitment, discuss it immediately with the direct report and negotiate a new commitment. Don't ignore your mistake.

PRAISE IN PUBLIC, CRITICIZE IN PRIVATE

Consistent recognition of your team strongly influences trust, primarily when it occurs in public and immediately after a goal or project has been met. Public praise and recognition of wins and individual/team successes create an energy of excellence. It allows others to learn by sharing best practices and motivates and energizes others to seek excellence.

Trusted leaders should always hold developmental conversations in private. The opportunity for a direct report to learn and grow from honest, open feedback is vital for their career and development. Still, it should never be discussed with other employees or shared with anyone other than the individual. Criticism can build a bridge of trust with your direct report as they learn you want to help them succeed.

CREATE ATTAINABLE CHALLENGES

To build rapport and trust with your team, assign projects that stretch each individual—delegate projects that are challenging and require work but are also achievable. Neuroscience has shown our brains enjoy accomplishing complex tasks. When moderate stress is experienced while working on a project, oxytocin is released, increasing focus and building team members' social connections. Difficult but attainable challenges should be considered "trust builders."

The projects must be attainable and always have an endpoint. When a project becomes extremely difficult or viewed by direct reports as impossible, it may cause them to give up on the task.

PROVIDE AUTONOMY

Autonomy in the workplace is a signal to your employees that you trust them. As often as possible, allow team members the autonomy to work independently and make their own decisions. The ability to be autonomous creates new and innovative ways of working. Individuals are more engaged and take greater accountability and personal responsibility when they feel they "own" a project or task. This has become increasingly relevant in a virtual work environment.

When a new leader promotes autonomy, it quickly highlights how everyone on the team is not the same and approaches work differently. As a result, creativity and innovation naturally emerge, creating a culture of mutual trust between staff and the manager.

Remember: A Manager Succeeds When Their Employees Succeed

When your team is successful, you are successful. When you have peak-performer employees, you will also be seen as a peak performer. Your employees' work and success are directly linked to yours, so do everything possible to help them succeed. Here are three suggestions to help that happen:

First, find out what barriers are stopping them from progressing and succeeding. Ask questions to ensure you understand, and then find ways to help them remove the obstacles. Let your team members do the work; your role is to clear the path and make it easier for them to work.

Second, provide the necessary resources for them to be successful. Do they need more time, additional people, or assistance with menial tasks? For example, as a new manager, I was responsible for an important training for senior leaders. I had two individuals assisting me in designing the training. When one of them was falling behind in their work, I asked why. He responded, "I didn't realize how long it would take to create this many PowerPoints." I was immediately angry at myself; I failed to recognize that I was using this brilliant individual to create slide decks instead of focusing him on the creation process.

Third, keep them motivated by acknowledging their wins. Everyone needs someone who is cheering them on at work and in life. Let them know when they do great work.

These three steps will help your team members be successful, which will help you succeed as a manager.

Key Takeaways

Building trust with your employees is essential to being a strong manager. Fostering trust with your direct reports builds a foundation of success and understanding between manager and direct report. Be sure and reread these key takeaways at least once a month to remind yourself how to build better relationships in the workplace:

→ Understand your organization's culture so you can build trust within the team.

→ Learn to identify the common reasons why employees distrust their managers, including lack of regular communication; disorganized, distant, or dishonest communication; unfair treatment; and arrogance and pride.

→ Take the time to self-reflect and discover your personal management style.

→ Implement the five strategies for creating rapport with your team: being authentic, keeping your word, praising in public and criticizing in private, creating attainable challenges, and providing autonomy.

→ When your team is successful, you are successful. Create success by removing employees' barriers to great work, providing the resources they need, and acknowledging their wins.

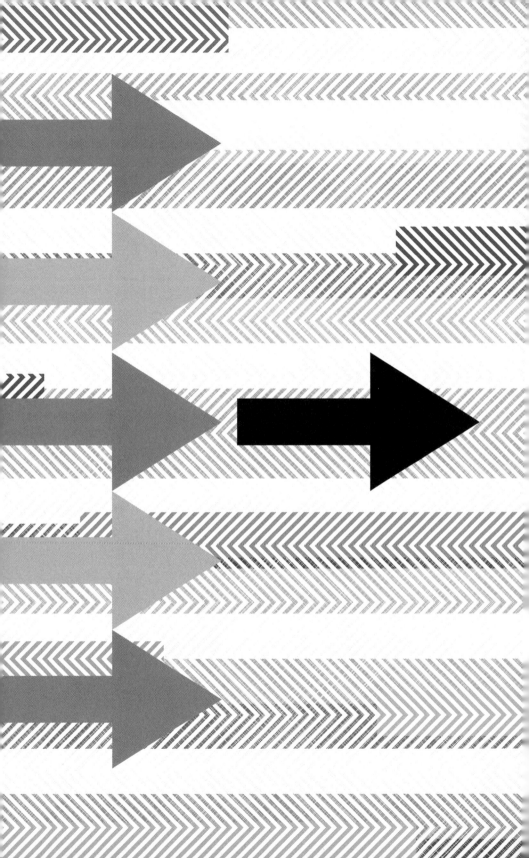

CHAPTER **4**

Creating a Positive Working Relationship with Your Superiors

If there is one individual in the organization you need a positive working relationship with, it is your boss. Your manager will have a significant impact and influence on your success. They have relationships and allies within the organization who can provide information and assistance crucial to your success. In addition, they have connections throughout the organization who can quickly integrate you into the organization and influence how you are perceived among the leadership team.

Being proactive in building a strong, positive relationship with your manager can be advantageous to your career and future within the organization. In order to create the right type of relationship with your boss, it is important to understand their personal management style. Learning to be flexible in meeting your manager's needs and the needs of your team is a crucial skill for new managers. Learning how to "manage up" or "manage your manager" will be a defining factor in your working relationship. If you don't know how to manage up, don't worry—I will provide all the necessary information, research, and steps to ensure your success.

Managing Up, Down, and All Around

Rachel was a standout from the moment I met her. She was promoted to a new position as a manager and joined our yearlong leadership-development program. During the first few sessions, Rachel took copious notes, engaged in the learning activities, and implemented what she learned in between sessions. However, during the fourth or fifth session, Rachel made a statement that was so impactful it changed the program: "In my short time as a new manager, I feel confident in my relationships with my direct reports and counterpart managers. Where I am struggling is learning how to interact with and, for lack of a better term, 'manage' my boss. I can't seem to get that part of the leadership equation right, and I need help."

Rachel's comment was a good one, but the room's reaction surprised me. Everyone nodded in agreement with a few outbursts of "me, too" and "I thought I was the only one." I immediately realized the mistake I had made by putting the topic of "managing up" at the end of the learning journey without much time devoted to the topic. Your relationship with your manager is as important as the one with your direct reports (if not more important!). Managers who effectively create a strong working relationship with their superiors and know how to manage them have access to information, resources, assistance, their network, and a host of other benefits—not to mention how nice it is to have a manager interested in developing you and helping you be successful.

The Responsibilities of a Manager to Their Boss

At the closing of a one-on-one with one of my direct reports, I asked him, "What can I do to help make you successful?" He responded, "I want to ask you the same question: What can I do to help make you successful?" I was shocked! I had never been asked that question before, and I liked it. That individual was taking responsibility for helping me be successful. Many of us spend time thinking about ourselves and worrying about our careers, but we may rarely think about one of the fundamental roles we play at work: making our manager successful.

First, it is your responsibility to get to know your manager and understand how they operate, communicate, coach, and make decisions. Do they like emails or instant messages? Long explanations or getting right to the point? Notice how your manager operates on a day-to-day basis.

Second, understand the goals of your manager. Of course, you are focused on reaching your target goals and having a great performance review, but don't forget you are there to assist and support your manager in attaining their goals. Seek to find out what your manager is accountable for.

Third, always, always, *always* meet your deadlines and, if possible, be early. If you think you will miss a deadline, immediately speak with your manager and let them know what is happening and why you are delayed.

How to Work with Your Boss Effectively

The relationship with your boss can be one of the most fulfilling and inspirational aspects of being a new manager. Managers who work well with their boss have improved job satisfaction, enjoy the support of senior employees, and participate in exciting new projects more often.

At one point, while working remotely, I rarely communicated with my boss. We were supposed to be checking in every month. After about two months, I realized I needed to increase how often I communicated with my boss, especially due to the feeling of being disconnected by remote work. I reached out to my boss and specifically listed what I felt would be helpful. I asked her how I could be a better employee and received feedback that included many valuable tips. After setting up weekly meetings, my connection to the workspace increased, my boss seemed to trust me more, and my trust in her flourished. The number of projects I participated in increased, and I was given more responsibility.

Having a healthy relationship with your boss allows the entirety of the organization to function better. Some ways to work with your boss more effectively are to come prepared to meetings, keep your boss informed, be considerate of their time, and stay open to their point of view. As you are proactive in your communication and thoughtfulness toward them, their trust in you will increase, and your overall job satisfaction will increase.

COME PREPARED

Time is one of the most precious resources in the workplace. To ensure a successful meeting with your boss, come prepared. Provide an update on your projects, aspects that need improvement, and possible solutions. Make a personal list of what you want to cover with your boss. If it is an issue, prepare several possible solutions to discuss. Preparation helps you appear responsible and trustworthy. Trust allows for a successful relationship.

KEEP THEM INFORMED

Few individuals like workplace surprises, and, most likely, your boss isn't one of them. Keeping your boss in the loop of what is occurring on your projects or work allows you to collaborate effectively. Frequent meetings build rapport and trust while allowing your boss to stay informed and keep other managers informed.

Keeping your manager informed includes discussing concerns, requesting assistance, and reporting work progress—the methods of keeping them informed range from in-person meetings to emails and phone calls. Be mindful of your boss's preference and keep them informed through their preferred method. These frequent and short meetings will help improve your relationship with your boss.

BE CONSIDERATE OF THEIR TIME

Anytime Justin walked into my office or called my cell, I knew the chat would last at least half an hour. Justin was an incredible employee, but one area he lacked was being considerate of others' time. Of course, you want to keep your boss informed and create a relationship of trust, but you can do both quickly, so you are considerate of their time.

When setting one-on-one meetings, inquire about what time works for them. Set a continuous meeting time on their schedule and ask how much time they have to meet. Keep the meetings concise, planned, and to the point. No one likes meetings that drag on. Have a clear purpose for the meeting, keep to the agenda, and do not spend time discussing topics that aren't of the utmost importance. Managers have busy schedules, and being considerate of their time will build a relationship of trust.

STAY OPEN TO THEIR POINT OF VIEW

As employees, we often think we understand the whole story or have a clear perspective on what is best for the company. As you come prepared to meetings and observe the workplace, understand your boss often has a bigger picture. Show respect for your boss's experience and position by staying open to their point of view, especially if it is different from your own.

FIGURE OUT THEIR TRIGGER POINTS AND MOTIVATORS

One of the most effective ways to work with your boss is to find out what things they like and don't like. It is that simple. Every manager has preferences in how they work, communicate, make decisions, motivate, coach, and provide feedback. Understanding their trigger points will help you avoid pitfalls that have the potential to make your manager angry or frustrated. You can learn a lot about your manager by viewing them and listening to their feedback.

Get to Know Your Boss's Working Style

I noticed a slight change in the facial expression of the manager the moment her direct report asked a question. When I asked the manager about it later, I found out it wasn't the content of the question that bothered her; it was how it was asked. "He doesn't seem to *get* how I work," she said. "In fact, he seems to do the opposite." A fascinating insight into the direct report is that he was a top producer, knew the market, and understood his clients.

The problem was that he didn't understand his manager, and it was hurting the relationship.

In twenty years of consulting, I have learned that it doesn't matter how knowledgeable you are, how much you sell, or how great you are at your job; if you don't know how to work well with your manager and understand their working style, you are at a disadvantage. Learning your manager's working style is not difficult; all you need is some old-fashioned detective work.

First, ask your manager about their working style, but provide specific context questions such as:

1. What is your communication style? How do you like to communicate and be updated on projects? And when in the workday is it the best time for these discussions?

2. What is the best way to ask for feedback and input?

Second, observe your manager in different settings. Find out:

→ How do they communicate?

→ How do they make decisions?

→ How do they manage situations?

→ How do they motivate others?

→ What causes them to get upset?

→ What gets them excited and engaged?

Learning the working styles of your manager will provide insight into how you can best work with them.

WHAT TO DO IF YOU'RE CLASHING WITH YOUR BOSS

There will come a time in your career when you won't get along with your boss. It happens to everyone, and it isn't a pleasant experience. If the clash and conflict continue for an extended period, that could have severe repercussions for your career—just ask me. I had a manager once tell me she "was going to do everything she could to fire me." Yes, even the author of this management book has clashed with his boss.

The good news is that you can take several actions to remedy the clashing. Identify where the disconnect, miscommunication, or misunderstanding occurs in order to understand the issue. By identifying the problem, you can take steps to mitigate the issue. Often the misconception is a difference in personal management or communication styles; the case may have nothing to do with you and have everything to do with not understanding each other.

Take a moment to self-reflect and see if you may be causing the problem. Maybe, in some small way, this clashing is due to *you*! Review your relationships with past managers and notice if you have had a conflict with most of your previous managers. Notice how you react to feedback, direction, or information you disagree with. If you are in conflict or arguing with your boss, you have already lost (and more than just the argument).

The Importance of Creating Alliances with Other Managers

As new managers, we have a strong instinct to prove our worth. This involves comparing our performance with that of other managers. Some do this by pointing out another's flaws and juxtaposing them with their strengths. Unfortunately, this strategy of competition often escalates to the tearing down of other managers and ultimately destroys any opportunity for a strong alliance with another manager.

Building relationships with other managers is key to your success. Solid relationships and alliances with other managers help you achieve your goals. They also allow the sharing of ideas and collaboration on issues. Strong alliances build a safety net around you; there is no better feeling than to know other managers have your back and want success for you as much as for themselves. The best managers know it is essential to create alliances with other managers from the start. Meet them, help them, and work with them.

If you help other managers accomplish their goals, it helps achieve your goals. If you want to advance to upper management, you'll need to build your reputation as a collaborator. This happens organically while working with other managers. The spirit of cooperation, unity, and even fun is available when we make alliances with other managers. Invest in the multidimensional benefits of creating alliances with your fellow managers.

30-DAY TIP: BUILD A NETWORK OF WELL-INFORMED COLLEAGUES

As you progress through your first few months of managing, you must begin building a network of well-informed colleagues. New managers focus on establishing routines, expectations, and relationships with their employees, and colleagues outside your immediate circle of responsibility may not be a priority. But those relationships should be, because networking is necessary in today's world. Research has shown your network leads to more job opportunities, career advancement, increase in status, and job satisfaction.

Your network should have a continual growth trajectory during your first year as a manager. You are designing a scaffolding from which you can access all levels of your organization. It will develop in strength and depth over time as you identify common interests, create friendships, and pay attention to others during your day's formal and informal moments. Even brief interactions may pay you back in dividends.

Several steps can help you build a strong network authentically. First, focus on common interests; finding individuals whose interests and goals align with yours is a good way to begin. Another way to build a network is by talking with and meeting as many individuals in the organization as possible. You never know when you will need advice or assistance from someone in another department who doesn't touch your work.

Finally, collaborating on projects, whether the time involved is extensive or short-term, builds teamwork, trust, and camaraderie.

5 Strategies for "Managing Up" When You Have a Difficult Supervisor

Managing up is one of the least discussed and most misunderstood topics in leadership and management development. Most leadership and management development is focused on the managers' direct reports and their interaction with them, such as holding one-on-ones, conducting performance reviews, and how to motivate, coach, and provide feedback. Yet, one topic that seems to be left out regularly is how to manage your manager.

This topic becomes even more critical when your manager is challenging to work with. But then, when the tables are turned, it is your responsibility to appropriately and tactfully manage your supervisor.

There are five crucial strategies for the skill of managing up. All of them can be learned and mastered through practice. Start by observing your supervisor's interactions to learn more about how they communicate, relate, provide feedback, and coach. Determine in what ways this is healthy versus unhealthy. Then, take time to reflect and reassess the situation. What is working, and what is not working? Take notes and plan how to discuss this with your manager.

Next, communicate your concern and ask questions to ensure you understand and have the information you need. Finally, anticipate their expectations. Learn what is and is not important to them and change your work output to match their priorities.

OBSERVE THEIR INTERACTIONS WITH OTHERS

To fully understand your boss and build the skill of managing up, you need to observe their interactions with others. Observing your manager allows you to understand your boss's management style. When interacting with your manager, be aware of what you hope to observe and home in on during these interactions.

For example, some bosses prefer to shower their employees with praise, but others do not. Some bosses prefer face-to-face contact, and others prefer emails. To work with your boss effectively, knowing how they want to interact, how they give (or do not give) praise, and their personalities allow you to set correct expectations. Likewise, this can allow you to notice what is working and what is not.

ASSESS WHAT ISN'T WORKING AND TAKE NOTES

When you are managing up, you must first self-reflect on what you are or aren't doing that contributes to the relationship with your boss. By taking time to understand what is negatively occurring in the workplace, you can make a fair, honest, and accurate judgment of your boss. This practice helps you respond to what isn't working and identify the areas that need improvement. Then, when giving feedback, refer to your list, which includes detailed and concise experiences that solidify your stance. Once those experiences have been recognized and noted, you can adequately create a plan to enhance the working relationship with your boss.

COMMUNICATE YOUR CONCERNS DIRECTLY

Discussing concerns and providing feedback to your boss can be difficult, scary, and tricky. Communicating concerns to a manager needs to be planned out. First, do your homework. Understand fully what you perceive your boss is doing wrong; when expressing concerns, show respect and humility while being polite and focused. Tell your boss what you need to succeed and focus on those specific aspects throughout the discussion. Do not take the conversation in a negative direction. For example, telling your boss they are a poor leader is counterproductive. When you go to your boss with a concern, always go with a solution in mind.

ASK QUESTIONS

When dealing with your boss and managing up, assuming is never a good route, especially about how or when they want to communicate. Always ask questions to get information and decipher what your manager wants or is asking for. These might include: "What is your workday like?" "What could I help with?" or "What are you worried about?" These questions will help you understand what is important to your boss so you can support them. When asking questions, find a good moment when they aren't stressed or rushed for time.

ANTICIPATE EXPECTATIONS

As you become well-acquainted with your boss's habits, communication style, and ways of motivating, anticipate their expectations. Good employees begin to expect requests and act accordingly. For example, if your boss wants updates on clients by one o'clock, do not wait to be asked for updates. Instead, send detailed notes early to avoid getting numerous requests about receiving the information.

Both Effective and Ineffective Managers Provide Learning Opportunities

A mantra that will serve you well is "I am either winning or learning." When individuals work with a problematic or ineffective manager, they often focus on the difficulties that arise from their situation. The focus is on "What I am not getting" or "How difficult the manager is to work with" rather than "What can I learn from this person that will help me in the future?"

I learned this lesson early on in my career. When I was promoted to manage a team, I was handed a key to a storage locker that contained all the equipment, reports, performance reviews, and leadership materials I would need for the position. Unfortunately, when I opened the storage locker, it was a chaotic mess.

The following day I came in jeans and a T-shirt and spent eight hours cleaning and organizing the storage unit. It was in pristine condition when my manager drove up. He asked me why I was not dressed for work and then proceeded to get upset that I was throwing out old documents from a decade prior. I was furious that, first, he had allowed the previous manager to leave everything a mess. Second, he did not recognize all my hard work in organizing important employee documents. At that moment, I realized I had learned a great lesson: how *not* to be a leader.

Often the lessons are just as poignant and important when they come from an ineffective manager as from an effective manager. So, watch your manager closely and learn from their example and mistakes.

Key Takeaways

The relationship with your manager can be one of the most fulfilling and enjoyable aspects of your job. To maintain this relationship, you need to have the skills and ability to manage the relationship. This includes knowing what your responsibilities to your manager are and how you can best work with them, so both of you are effective. Working effectively with your boss means you:

→ Come prepared

→ Keep them informed

→ Are considerate of their time

→ Stay open to their point of view

→ Figure out their trigger points and motivators

Managing your manager can be tricky. Learning how to appropriately manage up and maintain a strong relationship means you need to be able to:

→ Observe their interactions with others

→ Assess what isn't working and take notes

→ Communicate your concerns clearly

→ Anticipate their needs

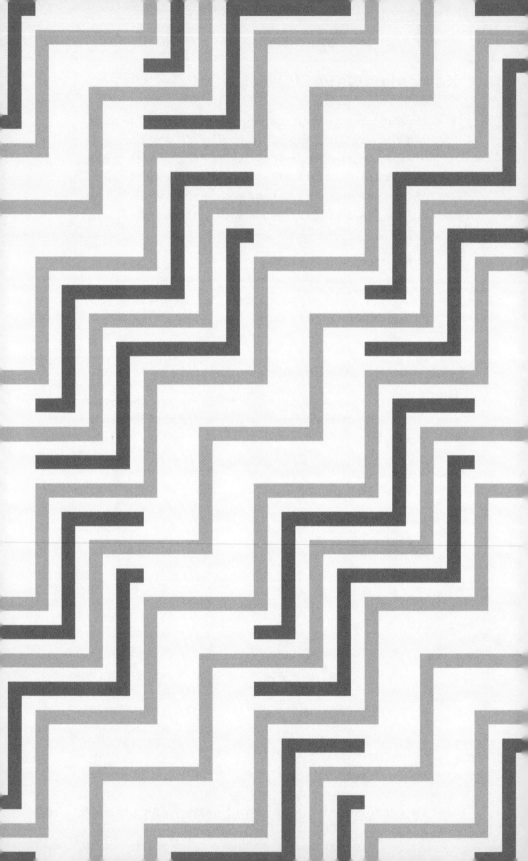

PART III

Your First 60 Days
Planning and Implementing Your Management Strategy

Congratulations! You have successfully maneuvered through your first thirty days as a new manager. In the first section of this book, you learned how to build relationships of trust. Next, you defined your management style and learned to manage change. As you enter the next thirty days, your focus will shift to planning and implementing a management strategy.

Successfully implementing your management strategy relies on understanding your team's strengths and weaknesses and how you, as their manager, can strategically use and maximize each team member's strengths. Successful managers motivate each team member to reach peak performance and project success.

As you identify the strengths and weaknesses of your team, you can set effective goals for each team member that contribute to the department's success. In addition, this information will allow you to draft a strategic plan and assign each member's role in that plan. Don't worry—by the time you finish this chapter, you will be prepared with the knowledge and tools you need to succeed in your first sixty days.

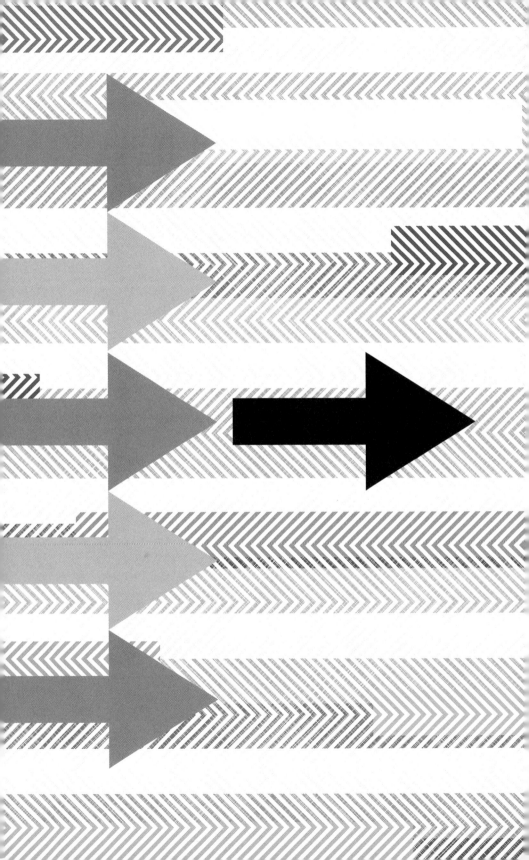

CHAPTER **5**

Identifying Your Team's Strengths and Weaknesses

I have always enjoyed watching sports fanatics. These individuals coach the players, scream at the referee, and tell the coaches what they should be doing. They are the experts and surely would win if they had the opportunity to have their voices heard. Unfortunately, most "couch coaches" don't completely understand the plays, the reason behind certain decisions, and the coaches' experience. They *think* they would do a great job, but in reality, they lack the expertise and information they would need to be successful.

This chapter will help you identify your team's strengths and weaknesses so you have the information you need to make good decisions, develop your people, and maximize performance. For managers, a key responsibility is assessing where your team is currently performing well and where it is not. Therefore, you need in-depth knowledge of the strengths and weaknesses at both the team and individual levels. This information maximizes your ability to plan and create strategies for success. In addition, it allows you to make good decisions about how and where you will use each team member and unlock their potential for growth and success.

Strengths vs. Weaknesses: A Manager's Dilemma

A gregarious, outspoken, and high-energy individual, Jenny was hired to increase sales, and she seemed to have all the qualities and skills needed to be successful. Her résumé was full of past successes, and she had relationships already built with key prospects. Yet, despite her past successes, Jenny struggled to close deals six months into her new position.

Jenny's manager joined in her sales calls and in-person meetings with customers to understand what was happening. It only took a few meetings for the manager to see Jenny's incredible strengths. She had strong relationships with her customers and already possessed a deep knowledge of the product. The customers liked her, and it showed in their conversations. However, Jenny also had a weakness that kept her from closing the sale: Her follow-up to client questions and requests was not timely or organized. As a result, the customer could not move forward with the product because they could not get the information, demonstrations, and pricing they needed in a timely manner.

Noticing Jenny's strengths in finding new clients, building solid relationships, and selling the product, her manager decided to increase the size of her territory to include more customers, and they provided her with a sales associate to handle the follow-up with her clients. Within weeks, deals began closing. By identifying Jenny's strengths and weaknesses, her manager provided her with a way to use those strengths while minimizing her shortcomings, and it ended up being a win for both Jenny and the team.

A Team Is Like a Winning Recipe

Managing a team is no simple task; creating a winning, success-ful team is even more difficult. It requires creating a strategic plan that incorporates set behaviors, communication, a collabora-tive culture, and a deep focus on the right priorities. In addition, successful teams embrace members' distinct strengths and per-sonality traits. Several ingredients need to be included to create a winning team:

1. Each team member needs to feel they play a substantial role in the team's success. Therefore, they need to be pro-vided with opportunities to use their strengths and grow and develop so they can build confidence in their skills and abilities.

2. Teams need strong leaders they can look to for guidance and assistance and who do not treat team members like subordinates but instead as valued contributors who are needed to be successful. In addition, they protect the team, creating a culture of trust.

3. Each team member must be responsible and reliable. Their role plays a part in the success of the larger group. A team member understands others depend on them.

4. Team members must consistently practice open commu-nication and feel comfortable voicing and working through differing opinions.

5. A strong team values the team win over individual success. They know the team, working together, can accomplish more than any individual.

60-DAY TIP: DO A DEEP DIVE INTO YOUR TEAM'S HISTORY

Your first few one-on-one meetings with your direct reports are the opportunity to:

- Begin the process of discovering their strengths and understanding their career goals

- Build trust

- Create a relationship as you learn more about each team member and their history on the team

- Set the right tone and expectations for future one-on-ones

Creating a trusting relationship by getting to know each team member's strengths, goals, and development areas can be overwhelming during initial one-on-ones. So don't bombard your direct report with questions; a one-on-one should not be an interrogation but rather a mutual sharing of information. A few suggested questions are:

- Do you have any favorite hobbies or other activities?

- How do you best like to communicate with other members of the team and me? (They may prefer live conversation with you but email their teammates, for example.)

- What are your career and development goals?

- What can I do to help you be successful?

- What has been your role on the team in the past?

- Why have you been successful in the past? What are some of your strengths that contributed to your success?

It is vital to know each team member to create a trusting relationship, but some questions are inappropriate to ask. Topics to stay away from include:

- Asking about race or ethnicity

- Asking if they are married or have a significant other

- Asking if they have children

- Asking their age

- Religious questions

The goal of a one-on-one is to get to know your employee, understand the history of the team and their role in that history and build a mutual relationship of trust while also learning more about how you can best work with them and help them be successful.

How to Balance Your Team's Strengths and Weaknesses

"Don't give that task to Dave; give it to Amy," a team member said during a delegation meeting of project tasks. "She will have it done in half the time and twice as good."

Everyone in the room laughed, including Dave, who said, "You're right. It isn't one of my strengths; it's one of my worst weaknesses."

The team members, who had been working together for more than a year, had identified their strengths and weaknesses. They held one another accountable to assign and accept tasks that were strengths and pass on tasks to others that were weaknesses, even if they were more high profile in nature. When I asked the manager about it after the meeting, she said, "I don't need to speak up 95 percent of the time; when assigning project tasks, the team is fully aware of one another's strengths and weaknesses."

Every person has strengths and weaknesses. The idea is to balance these among a team so each team member is doing work they are great at to ensure a productive and successful outcome.

ASK YOUR TEAM TO REFLECT ON THEIR SKILLS

Everyone within a team needs to be aware of areas in which they excel, perform best, and thrive. Knowing their strengths increases self-awareness and the ability to identify where they can provide the most benefit to a project or team. Ask your team to reflect on their areas of expertise, strengths, and where they believe they excel. Provide team members time to think, self-reflect, and ask others for input. Encourage them to write down their responses and schedule a time to discuss their findings. Listen intently during the discussion to learn more about each team member.

LOOK AT YOUR TEAM'S PAST PERFORMANCE

You can learn about the team and each member by reviewing past performance to gain insight into strengths and weaknesses. As you do this, ask "Why?" It is important to analyze why things went poorly and why they went well, and who contributed to each outcome. Likewise, pay attention to tasks the team completed that went well or poorly. This is a strong insight into their strengths and weaknesses. As you analyze an individual's work on a project, consistency among the identified strengths and weaknesses will emerge. Note these outcomes and make decisions accordingly.

OBSERVE INDIVIDUAL SUCCESSES AND LOSSES

Being attentive and engaged with each team member is vital as a manager. When working daily with the same people, a manager can fall into a habit of focusing on tasks and goals and getting things done. As a result, it becomes difficult to observe team members' strengths and weaknesses daily. Not being aware of everyone's specific hand in successes and losses is a missed opportunity. Instead, pay attention to team members' strengths and weaknesses, and their influence on success and failures. Write down what you learn and compare it to overall patterns to fully understand each team member's strengths and weaknesses.

GAUGE CONSISTENCY AROUND CERTAIN TASKS

With so much to do as a manager, it can be challenging to observe performance patterns, behaviors, and successes/failures over time. Often there is a lag between the behavior or action and the result. To fully grasp an individual's consistency of strengths, behaviors, and results, watch for patterns over time. For example, if an individual is regularly in charge of a specific task and is performing well, a good manager understands that team member has the skills needed to succeed in that role. Likewise, if a team member frequently struggles with a particular task, that skill set may be a part of their weaknesses. Adjust team member roles to reflect the information gathered.

BE UPFRONT AND HONEST

After you ask your team members to reflect on their skills, strengths, and weaknesses, they will be interested in your viewpoint and observations on this topic. Be honest and up front with your answer. Provide specific examples to back up your viewpoint. Give the gift of being honest so employees can take the opportunity to develop and improve. Create an environment of trust and development where you identify their strengths and weaknesses.

Is Your Employee Underperforming or Are Structural Issues at Fault?

When an employee has a performance issue, it is difficult for both them and the manager. Before jumping to conclusions or accepting information from fellow colleagues, it is vital to understand what is at the root of the employee's poor performance. Asking a few questions of the individual and taking the time to think about the answers will provide you with the information needed to discover whether the employee is the cause or if the organization needs to make changes.

1. Does my direct report have all the information, training, and ability to do this task?

2. Are the specific tasks and expectations straightforward for my direct report?

3. Is there a process in place they need to know about? Or have they not followed the process?

4. Is there an organizational obstacle or other barrier hindering the employee from completing the task?

5. What are the causes of the poor performance, both individually and organizationally?

Be sure to listen intently and ask questions to clarify the information they provide.

Managers can make the faulty assumption they understand why an employee is underperforming and quickly jump to resolve the issue. Instead, investigate the reasons for the performance issues, gathering as much information as possible. Understanding the role that organizational processes play, along with individual issues, will help the manager provide feedback and coaching.

Immerse Yourself in Your Company's Processes and Systems

I have always enjoyed people-watching at Walt Disney World. (With six kids, I go there more than I'd like to admit!) It is quickly apparent who has been to the Magic Kingdom before and who has not. Those who know Disney World understand you have to race to certain rides first, and if you get there quick enough, you can ride them several times. They know how to use their lightning lane pass (fast-pass system) and when and where you should eat lunch to avoid long lines. These Disney experts understand the system; they have a process and get the most out of their day with Mickey Mouse.

The same idea goes for your company. As a manager, it is vital to understand your organization's processes and systems, and have a relationship with individuals involved in those areas. The more you know and understand your organization, the better equipped you are to help your team and influence change. It isn't *what* you know, it's *who* you know—having a relationship, even if only an acquaintanceship, with individuals in other departments can help when you need something or have a question.

For example, when one of my direct reports' bonuses wasn't right, I took it to my manager, who did the same with his manager, and the response came back that everything was correct. However, I knew the numbers and the accounts that had purchased products, and the reports told a different story. So, I called a friend I had met on a company award trip years before who worked in the payroll/bonus department. We stayed in touch infrequently but still were friendly. I explained the situation and my reports, and he said he would look into it. Within a day, I received a call back that we were right, the purchase hadn't shown up yet, and my sales rep would receive her bonus next quarter. I was glad I understood the process and knew someone I could call. Be the manager who has relationships throughout the whole organization.

5 Strategies for Maximizing Your Team's Strengths

A key aspect of business success is helping develop your employees' strengths and using those strengths to carry out the goals and mission of the company. Everyone brings a specific skill set to the team that, when capitalized upon, can create a strong working unit. The diversified skills of each person need to be recognized and built upon. As a good manager creates projects, assigns roles, and puts employees on similar teams, they are mindful of individual strengths and how they can best use them.

Five strategies to help maximize your team's strengths are encouraging them to self-assess, aligning their responsibilities with the expectation of the role, giving them a sense of ownership, helping co-workers learn and understand one another's strengths, and allowing and encouraging employees to develop weaknesses into strengths. When you leverage these strengths, productivity and effectiveness increase and employees enjoy more ownership and success. Instead of focusing on weaknesses, good managers focus on building team strengths and acting as a mentor to promote career growth.

ENCOURAGE THEM TO SELF-ASSESS

We live with ourselves every day. We intimately know our strengths and weaknesses, and unfortunately, our focus is usually on what we are not good at or where we are failing. Self-assessing what we are good at and areas that need improvement is essential for employee development and team success. Encourage your team to self-assess by assigning them to perform a strengths, weaknesses, opportunities, and threats (SWOT) analysis, which creates self-awareness of their perceived qualities. Prompt them to be specific in each of these categories. Once completed, ask them to analyze how they can maximize their outlined strengths and minimize their weaknesses. Also, encourage employees to take advantage of opportunities and be mindful of possible threats to success.

ALIGN THEIR RESPONSIBILITIES WITH THE EXPECTATIONS OF THEIR ROLE

One of the top ten complaints by employees is that their responsibilities do not align with their role, or their responsibilities shifted as time progressed on the job. To ensure this does not occur, pay attention to the functions and assignments each individual is given in a project. Then, delegate the correct assignments to the departments or individuals who were hired for and are best trained for that role. In doing this, you ensure each employee uses their strengths and specialized skills.

GIVE THEM A SENSE OF OWNERSHIP

Autonomy and ownership are strong motivators for success. Research has shown that when employees are provided autonomy and ownership over projects, they are more proactive in their job roles and assume more responsibility for their work. Employees who have ownership are more dedicated to the outcome of a project or task; they care about the organization and produce better work. To help employees feel ownership, ask for the team's input on work matters. Empower them with the responsibility of having a say in projects or processes. Do not micromanage. Micromanaging erodes any sense of ownership or independence individuals may develop. Instead, offer help or guidance and resist the urge to fix things.

HELP CO-WORKERS LEARN AND UNDERSTAND ONE ANOTHER'S STRENGTHS AND WEAKNESSES

Peer-to-peer learning embeds knowledge and helps an effective team become more cohesive. Creating teams and projects based on the unique strengths of each team member is a positive way to help the organization achieve its larger goals. Encourage team-building activities where each team member can identify their strengths and the strengths of other team members. Once each team member understands the others' strengths, they can delegate and work with one another to build both the individual and the team.

ALLOW AND ENCOURAGE EMPLOYEES TO DEVELOP WEAKNESSES INTO STRENGTHS

Putting employees in a position or a role that builds their strengths is essential, but it is also vital to help employees turn their weaknesses into strengths. Career development is a crucial motivator for employees. One way to develop a weakness includes pairing the employee with another individual who has a strength in that area. Another way is in a controlled situation such as a training meeting. Choose topics that are weaknesses of the team and provide meaningful feedback and encouragement that bolster it. Finally, create a safe environment for employees to make mistakes and learn from them.

Empower Your Employees to Innovate

Now more than ever, innovation is a vital skill for employees. We are in a hyper-novel society where change is happening at a rate unseen at any time in human history. Cultivating a culture of innovation ensures you stay ahead of your competitors.

As a manager, the following essential leadership strategies will build a culture of innovation in your team:

Encourage dialogue and allow for failure. No one gets it right the first time. We need to create a workplace where people feel safe to try new ideas. Often innovative efforts don't work on the first try. When employees know their manager will give space for a creative idea that might not work on the first try, they will be encouraged to keep innovating.

Brainstorm together. Collaborate and brainstorm with employees and let them know you value their contribution and are willing to engage in their efforts. This can be a weekly strategy meeting or an informal one-on-one.

Act on ideas. The number one way to kill innovation is to never implement or act on employee ideas. Instead, show trust by brainstorming and vetting their ideas, and implement them when something looks like it might work.

Key Takeaways

This chapter did a deep dive into the human aspect of management and the importance of knowing the strengths and weaknesses of each team member. Be sure and reread these key takeaways at least once a month to remind yourself how to identify, build, and use the strengths and diminish or rebuild the weaknesses of your direct reports.

→ Understand how to identify your team's strengths and weaknesses.

→ Get to know the history of each of your direct reports.

→ Know how to balance your team's strengths and weaknesses on important projects and tasks.

→ Take steps to understand if an employee is under-performing; decipher whether it is an employee skill issue or an organization process issue.

→ Know the five strategies for maximizing your team's strengths:

- Encourage them to self-assess

- Align their responsibilities with the expectation of their role

- Give them a sense of ownership

- Help co-workers learn and understand one another's strengths and weaknesses

- Allow and encourage employees to develop weak-nesses into strengths

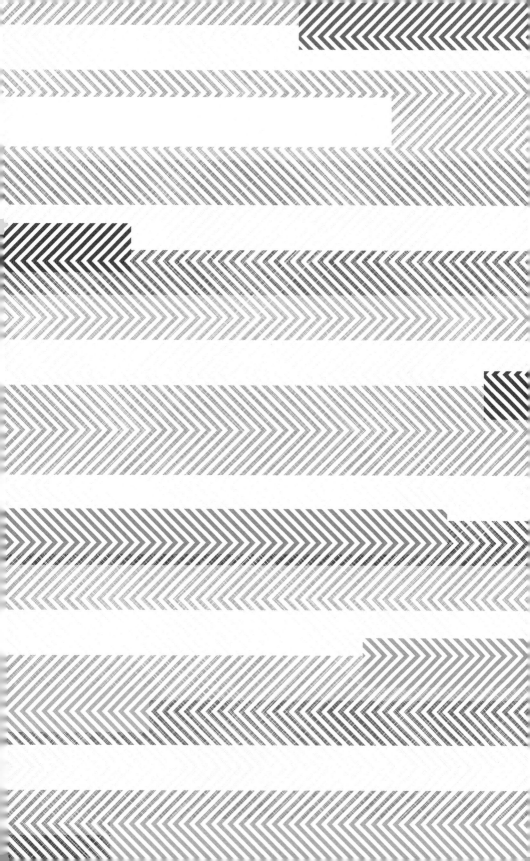

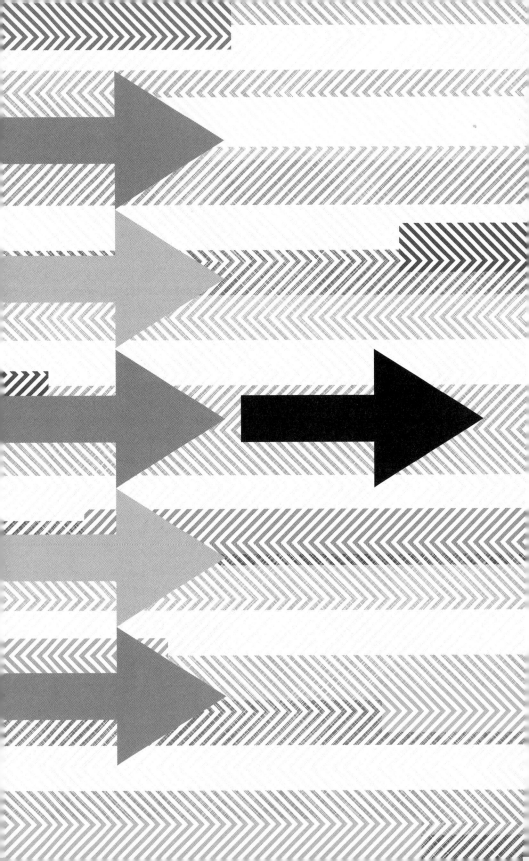

CHAPTER **6**

Creating Actionable Goals and a Strategic Plan

A symphony, a cure for a disease, an innovative product, a book of stunning photographs, and the experience of a lifetime. What do all of these have in common? Nearly every great accomplishment a human has achieved is due to a plan that was put in place with achievable goals. Strategic plans that include measured goals are the recipe for success and the formula for accomplishment, yet they are difficult for individuals to achieve. We often hear of failed diets, failed attempts at writing a book, and projects that didn't meet client expectations. With all the current research available, why do so many individuals and organizations fail to meet their strategic goals and plans? I answer that question in this chapter and give you the tools and skills you need to create actionable goals and a strategic plan. Your goals and strategic plan are not accomplished through big, massive actions. Instead, they heavily depend on doing small things every day that compound over time to build positive habits.

How Small Goals Won the Tour de France

For one hundred years, the British were considered mediocre professional cyclists. From 1908 to 2004, British cyclists won only a single gold medal at an Olympic Games. No British cyclist had ever won the Tour de France. David Brailsford was hired to change that. Brailsford and his team of coaches laid out a plan with clear, actionable goals to make small adjustments in every possible area of cycling. They redesigned the bike seats, tested various fabrics in a wind tunnel to increase aerodynamic flow, and even painted the inside of the vehicle that carried the bikes white, so they could see any bits of dust that could degrade the performance of the bikes.

Brailsford focused on small daily goals that, over time, would significantly affect his team's performance. He was right, and research has since substantiated his plan. Only five years after Brailsford took over, the British cycling team dominated the road and track cycling events at the 2008 Olympic Games in Beijing. Four years later, the Brits raised the bar at the Olympic Games in London as they set nine Olympic records and seven world records. The very same year, David Brailsford and the British cycling team accomplished the Mount Everest of cycling goals when Bradley Wiggins became the first British cyclist to win the Tour de France. His teammate Chris Froome won the next year and again in 2015, 2016, and 2017. The British won five Tour de France victories in six years. How did this happen? A strategic plan, when combined with small, attainable goals that are implemented daily, will result in improvement. The general belief that massive success requires massive action is untrue. The magic happens through daily activities that may seem to make no difference when looked at from a day-to-day point of view, but when you look back over a year or two, the results will be strikingly apparent.

Success Is Contingent upon Your Knowledge of Company Goals

While on a client visit with an experienced salesperson, I was repeatedly surprised when he focused the conversation on a third-tier product instead of our flagship one. The bonus structure was low for their choice and the new product carried a more significant bonus potential. After three customer visits, I asked him why his primary focus during the sales call wasn't on the flagship product. He said he had a large customer base who used the older product and switching them to the newer product would be difficult.

It was clear to me at that moment he didn't understand the company goals for this product line. The older product would soon be retired, so he had limited time to switch his clients. The newer product also paid more in bonuses to incentivize the salespeople to make the switch. Somehow during our team meetings, this individual had misheard or misunderstood the new company goals. Focusing on the wrong area was costing him money and a possible future promotion.

It is important to align individual and team goals with the organization's goals. This ensures both internal and external clients hear the same message the organization delivers. Also, resources are created or distributed around organizational goals. Ensure your team members' goals are stacked on organizational goals for consistent alignment.

How to Set Effective Goals for Your Team

I would be willing to wager that all you have accomplished over the years is a result of effective goals that were achieved through compounded habits. Setting effective goals is the key to both individual and team success. When building good habits, managers must set effective team goals. To make effective changes, first set specific goals that create a target the team can aim for. Once a vision has been established, employees must set daily actions that align with the individual's and organization's visions and goals. Research shows that goals are more likely to be achieved when they are small instead of massive, and don't overwhelm and burn out team members. Don't doubt the power of small goals; small actions compound to significant change and accomplishments. Each small daily action moves us closer to our goals and changes us as individuals. Instead of focusing on what you want to achieve, focus on what you want to become.

IDENTIFY A SPECIFIC GOAL YOU WANT TO ADDRESS OR TARGET YOU WANT TO REACH

Goal setting is a powerful process that, when used correctly, can propel positive change and achievement. The first step is to identify a specific goal. This overall target and vision provide direction for each step in the goal-setting process. Next, outline a goal that is clear, well-defined, and measurable. Finally, choose a quantifiable goal so progress can be benchmarked and therefore be impactful. Avoid goals that are not specific, well-defined goals, such as "I will provide better service for my clients." This is not a specific, well-defined goal. Instead, reframe your goals in a proactive, straightforward manner, such as "I will take thirty minutes per day to stop and review my work and ensure I am providing excellent service to my clients.

MAKE IT A SMALL GOAL

Researchers who study self-control and self-discipline define willpower as a muscle strengthened through practice. A common misstep in setting goals is choosing a goal that is too difficult or out of the weight limit your self-control muscle can lift. Set a small goal that helps you become 1 percent better each day while not causing burnout. Small habits should not be underestimated. Research has found small goals completed daily have a much higher likelihood of success.

CREATE SPECIFIC, ACTIONABLE PLANS TO ACCOMPLISH YOUR GOAL

Once you have identified your goal, you need to create specific, actionable steps to reach it. First, write down the steps required to accomplish your objective. Next, break down your goal into manageable chunks with specific deadlines. These should reflect what needs to be done daily, weekly, and monthly to reach your goal. Once you have identified the actions to be taken, write them into your daily schedule so you know what you need to do every day, week, and month. Writing it down lets you see how much time you need to allow for each small milestone. Continue to adjust your goals based on what your daily and weekly schedule looks like. Be sure to be flexible and, when possible, get ahead. Life is always full of surprises that may take time out of your schedule.

HABITS COMPOUND OVER TIME

In his famous book *Atomic Habits*, James Clear states, "You get what you repeat." The actions you take each day compound consistently into significant changes and habits. You do not gain thirty pounds over the course of a week (outside of a medical issue); gaining weight is the outcome of compounded eating habits. Compounded action, both good and bad, can create tremendous change and accomplishment or hinder your success. Instead of overwhelming large changes that cause burnout, focus on small, positive changes that produce stronger habits over time. Unfortunately, our brains seek large changes instead of realizing the power of compounding behaviors to create long-term success.

FOCUS ON WHO YOU WANT TO BE, NOT JUST WHAT YOU WANT TO ACHIEVE

When we change and develop as adults, our identities also change. Our habits grow out of the identity we create for ourselves. How we view ourselves, both the negative and the positive, informs how we act and what habits we defer to. To make lasting change, identify who you want to be, not just what you want to do or accomplish. Invest time in creating your "ideal self," or the identity you want to become. What is that individual like? Instead of wanting to be a person who reads more, acquire the identity of a reader. Your identity is not set in stone, and it will change as you choose habits that align with your ideal self. Research has shown this is one of the best ways to sustain habits.

COMMON REASONS WHY BUSINESS GOALS AREN'T MET

Whether it be to avoid ice cream past 6 p.m., write another chapter for my book, or complete the next phase of a client project, I always have positive intentions to meet my goals because I know they will benefit the team, the organization, and me personally. But like most of us, I sometimes don't meet my business or personal goals. Unfortunately, the reasons we don't succeed are more common than people realize:

► The goal loses its importance, or we personally change. For example, a manager may value employee development and strongly encourage the team to participate in monthly courses. However, when the manager is promoted or leaves the organization, the importance of personal development decreases.

► We don't have a clear plan with specific steps to mark our progression.

► We get busy! We may take on too much work, or deadlines on other projects are quickly approaching and our time to work toward our goal is limited.

► We get distracted. I call this "life happens." This is when Aunt Jane comes to visit for two days but stays for three weeks, a family member becomes ill, or a significant other gets a promotion, so we take on more responsibilities at home. Life is full of unexpected twists and turns that may distract us from achieving our goals.

► We often set goals that are too big, and when we don't feel like we are progressing, we become overwhelmed and unmotivated.

Immerse Yourself in Your Company's Financials

There is a general belief that if your role is not in a financial management position, it isn't essential to have a complete understanding of the company's financials. That is untrue. It is in your best interest to have a full understanding of the financial side of the organization. A lot of information can be gained from understanding an organization's financials as a leader and employee. Let me provide an example.

As a new leader, I received advice from my manager to look at the company's quarterly financials. At first, I didn't know how to read the report, let alone understand it. I asked for assistance from a mentor, and within a few months I had a general understanding of the report. During a market downturn, I noticed that certain numbers were changing, which alerted me to the fact the organization was not making the same amount of money it previously had while it was also spending more to acquire customers. I knew if this trend continued, it might lead to organizational restructuring or layoffs. This inspired me to dive deeper into the reports and ask questions. Unfortunately, I was right; several months later, the organization made budget cuts and stopped hiring new employees. This is only one example of the information you can glean from understanding your company's financials. You will be a better leader if you know and can interpret them.

You should be familiar with and know how to analyze three types of financial statements:

- A **balance sheet** provides a snapshot of the company's financial health for a particular time period.

- A **cash flow statement** details the inflows and out-flows of cash.

- An **income statement** (profit and loss) offers an over-view of income and expenses during a specific period.

By talking to your finance manager, you can clearly understand these financial statements and get a full view of the company's financial health. You can use this infor-mation and bring value to your role by sharing what you learn and showing the impact of your team's work on the organization.

5 Strategies for Creating a Strategic Plan for Your Team or Department

There is an old aphorism that goes, "Give me six hours to chop down a tree, and I will spend the first four sharpening the knife." Preparing and planning to be successful as a company provides a sense of direction and outlines the primary goals, opportunities, and threats that play a prominent role in the health of a company. Then, as each department's smaller goals work toward the company's larger strategic goals, the company runs like a well-oiled machine.

According to research outlined in the *Harvard Business Review*, 85 percent of executive leaders spend less than one hour per month discussing strategy, and 50 percent spend no time at all. In turn, 90 percent of businesses fail to meet their strategic targets. Therefore, we can conclude that strategic planning must be executed to ensure an organization can reap the rewards of a proper business strategy. To create a successful strategic plan, review the global or company-wide strategic plans. Then, pay attention to the internal and external business factors that influence strategy. Once the team has a good understanding of these factors, it can determine the area of focus and create strategies around that focus.

REVIEW GLOBAL OR COMPANY-WIDE STRATEGIC PLANS

To write up an effective team strategic plan, a manager must first understand the overall company-wide strategic plans. Being well versed in organizational strategy allows the manager to create cohesive team plans with the larger corporate vision. Each company has defined goals; most extend five to ten years into the future. Global or company-wide plans can cover a wide array of aspects. Search out the company's revenue goals, product goals, people goals (diversity and inclusion), and/or expansion goals. Home in on what aspects are most important for your team.

ANALYZE EXTERNAL BUSINESS FACTORS

External business factors are a crucial input for strategy formulation. External analysis means examining the industry environment around a company. This includes paying attention to what the market is doing, the competitive structure, pricing, and the industry's history. Analyzing these external business factors determines the opportunities or threats that might present themselves. Awareness of external factors will drive strategic planning, growth, and volatility. Likewise, external factors can include market segments or distinct groups of customers that drive specific demands. Each of these demographics and behaviors are important considerations.

ANALYZE INTERNAL BUSINESS FACTORS

Internal factors refer to anything within the organization that will affect business—mastering and knowing about internal factors impact how you, as a manager, can control and adjust for them. Strategic planning can mitigate or capitalize on the factors affecting the company. Unlike external factors, a company can control internal factors. Internal factors may be the role of company leadership, the management style, the strength of the employees in certain areas, innovation, and financial health. Also, pay attention to both negative and positive company culture.

DETERMINE YOUR AREA OF FOCUS

Once you completely understand the internal plans and external factors, determine an area of focus that will be the foundation of your strategy. This should expand on your company role and how it aligns with the team and organizational strategic plans. Regardless of your area of work or position in the company, the focus should be on how your work affects the client and the organization's success. For example, staying sales/customer-client focused is essential even if you work in finance logistics. Link your role and the work you do to client success and organizational growth and success. Also, choose your number of focus areas based on what your team can realistically focus on at one given time. Do not overload team members.

BRAINSTORM

Once you have reviewed company strategic plans and analyzed external factors, it is important to brainstorm before drafting your strategic plan. Whether you brainstorm together as a group or independently, research highly recommends brainstorming. Brainstorming allows ideas to be brought up and triggers more ideas. Seek to break the routine of organizational processes and systems and allow for out-of-the-box thinking that can be reimagined to fit the strategic plan. Brainstorming provides fresh ideas and helps filter current ideas to ensure workability.

Drafting a Successful Strategic Plan

Writing a strategic plan is not a one-person job. You, as the manager, may be the one to write it physically, but to be successful you will need the input of several other individuals. An effective plan is vital for organizational and team success because it aligns everyone with a common goal. Your plan is only as successful as the information informing the content.

Include upper management or other leaders to whom you are accountable. They have a broad view of your team's needs, and securing their buy-in is crucial to creating an effective plan. It is critical to be clear on the organization's mission and vision. Often other leaders in the company have information about the industry, competitors, or market trends that will shape the execution of your plan. Include people from different departments and levels. Gather as much data as possible to provide insight into the direction your team needs to be headed. Collaboration is key to a great plan.

With a collaborative and data-driven vision in mind, focus on the goals and priorities that will help you achieve it. Define objectives and initiatives that advance your plan. The goals you create should not be so big or broad that they are overwhelming. Be realistic about what can be accomplished, so your team has an achievable vision. Track your success monthly and celebrate often with your team. Realign when needed.

Presenting Your Proposal to Your Boss

When presenting a strategic plan to a leader, you should consider several tactics to ensure it is communicated correctly. First, don't rely on written communication alone. Ask for an in-person meeting to clarify any misconceptions. You should email the plan before the meeting so your manager can review it. Include visuals when discussing your plan; this could include graphs or PowerPoints. Everyone learns and processes information differently, so have both visual and written information.

Be ready and willing to receive feedback. At this point, your boss should have played a role in creating the plan, but when it's presented as a whole, they will likely have some input or suggested adjustments. Be ready and willing to accept criticism, learn, and make changes if needed. Your job is to present your vision for your team in a clear and informed way.

Key Takeaways

This is one of the most important chapters in the book as we prepare you for your first ninety days as a manager. It is vital to understand how to set effective goals for your team, learn about your organization's finances, and have the tools to create a strong strategic plan. This will help ensure your success and make you stand out among other leaders. Be sure to reread this chapter's key takeaways at least once a month:

→ Know how to set effective goals for your team.

- Identify a specific goal you want to address or target you want to reach.

- Make the goal small.

- Create specific, actionable plans to achieve your goal.

- Habits compound over time.

- Focus on whom you want to be, not just what you want to achieve.

→ Understand your company's financials.

→ Know the five strategies for creating a strategic plan for your team or department.

- Review global or company-wide strategic plans.

- Analyze external business factors.

- Analyze internal business practice.

- Determine your area of focus.

- Brainstorm.

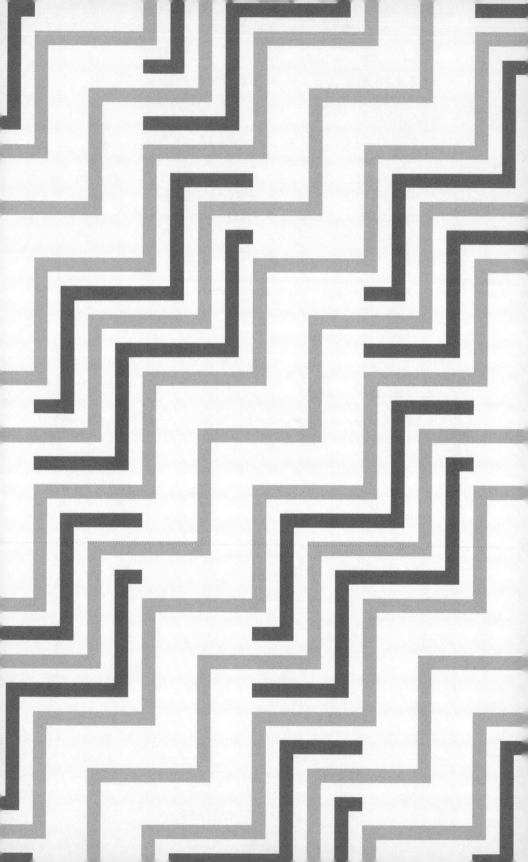

PART IV

The First 90 Days
Learning How to Refine, Pivot, and Troubleshoot

Leadership is about humanity. Everyone has successes, failures, and everything in between. There is no perfect leader, just as there is no perfect employee.

As a new salesperson right out of college on the first day working with my boss, I was excited to wear one of two new suits I had recently purchased. I left the house looking sharp and ready to take on the world. However, during my first sales call, my manager looked at me with a large grin while I was selling my product.

After we finished and walked out to the car, my boss said, "Chris, raise your right hand." Thinking he had lost his mind, I did as he asked and quickly noticed all the tags for my new suit were hanging from my right sleeve. I was so embarrassed.

He smiled and said, "Chris, you will look back on this situation in a few years and laugh. You will do a great job and be successful, just remember you are human and will make mistakes along the way." This section focuses on people—how to motivate employees, provide difficult feedback, and manage expectations.

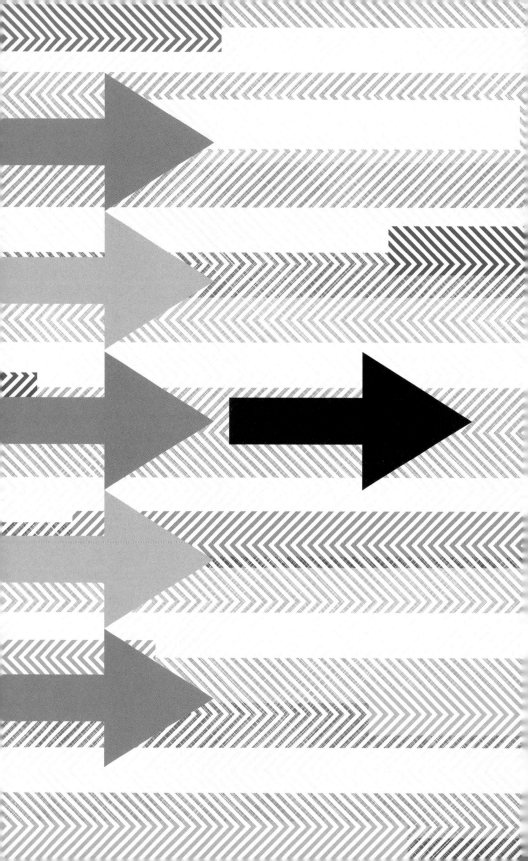

CHAPTER 7

Navigating Difficult Employees and Poor Performance

One of the best aspects of being a manager is helping employees navigate difficult times, poor performance, and development issues. Yes, you read that correctly. Helping employees get back on track, improve performance, and change behaviors is one of the most satisfying (and challenging) responsibilities you will have as a leader. Out of everything you do as a manager, one of the most significant contributors to your legacy is how you help employees through difficult times.

To prepare and provide you with the tools you need, I will cover the most effective ways you, as a manager, can help employees succeed. I will also review the common reasons employees can be challenging to work with and what factors contribute to these behaviors. Learning how to share difficult but developmental feedback is crucial to your success. This chapter will prepare you for one of the most exciting and complex aspects of being a manager.

Self-Pity, Poor Performance, and Personal Progress

Tony was having a difficult year. He had been recognized as a top performer in previous years, but after being placed on a high-profile, fast-moving, and labor-intensive new project, Tony was underperforming. Tony expressed to his manager why he was not at fault for the project's status and his poor performance. He then asked to be taken off the project. Tony's manager listened intently, took notes, and decided to get more information before providing any coaching or making judgments.

After meeting with project team members to gather feedback, the manager learned that everyone felt Tony was a problem; without him, the project would be successful. Some of their feedback included:

▸ He doesn't update the team on the progress of his work, which holds back its ability to progress.

▸ He isn't a team player. Instead, he seeks out work that is visible to leadership and wants nothing to do with anything he considers below his role.

▸ He worries only about himself, and the team doesn't trust him.

At their next meeting, Tony's manager addressed the problems and provided specific examples. At first, Tony was defensive, but as his manager discussed his attitude, lack of communication with the team, and seeking out the spotlight, Tony began to see his contribution to the project's failure.

It was a difficult conversation for both parties and spanned several meetings. Then, focusing on how to progress and change, they worked together to devise a plan to help turn the project around and change Tony's behaviors and perceptions. Of course, the change didn't occur overnight, but Tony worked hard to incorporate the feedback, and the project was completed successfully.

Helping Employees Succeed Is Key to Being a Successful Manager

"I can't do this!" I have heard this phrase hundreds of times in my career, and more than 95 percent of the time, the individual saying it was wrong. They *could* do it—with work, effort, determination, and grit. A new project, a new skill, a new position presents itself, and the first thing your brain does is think of all the ways you won't be successful. It identifies the barriers and goes to work to convince you this will be harder than you think, you don't have the skills, and this new endeavor is nearly impossible.

A manager can change that thinking. When you share with your employee that you see their potential and they will be successful with hard work and effort, it changes how they think. Sometimes we need someone to tell us we can do something when we don't believe we can. It kicks in one of the best human emotions we have: hope.

After giving up her career and staying home to raise our six children, my wife decided to return to school. She applied to the local community colleges and universities. While discussing it one day, I asked her if she had thought about attending an Ivy League school like Harvard for her master's degree. She responded that she had never thought about it: "I am a small-town girl from southern Alberta, Canada. I don't know one person from my town who has gone to an Ivy League school." "Well, you can be the first," I told her, and I encouraged her throughout the application process. A short three years later, she not only graduated with a master's from Harvard, but she was also a teaching fellow for three courses. I knew she could do it, even when she didn't. The same goes for your employees—they may not realize they can do it, but you know they can, so encourage them to try. All it takes is for you to help them start their journey, overcome barriers, and cheer them on. It is an impactful experience; those individuals will tell their grandchildren about how you helped them succeed.

Common Reasons Why Employees Are Difficult to Work With

While speaking at a conference, I showed a slide listing ten issues all managers face. Then, I asked the participants to choose one from the list they felt represented the most challenging responsibility of a manager and enter that into the handheld responders we had given them at the beginning of the presentation. Overwhelmingly, more than 70 percent of the audience responded that managing difficult and underperforming employees was the most challenging aspect of their role. Unfortunately, managers consistently deal with this issue throughout their careers. Therefore, recognizing and managing difficult employees is a vital skill for a successful manager. To prepare you to deal with difficult employees, I have created a list of the common reasons they are challenging to deal with.

RESISTANCE TO CHANGE

Organizational change is a constant in the new world of work. It has become a natural and needed process to improve business results, increase revenue, and work with clients. Unfortunately, employees' resistance to change produces issues for the company, team, and themselves. Typical results of resistance to change include project delays, loss of revenue, and decreased morale. In addition, skeptical attitudes and conversations around change can make these employees challenging to work with because these negative views can reduce motivation and, more importantly, hinder the team's and the organization's progress.

POOR ATTITUDE

"Don't be a downer," my mother used to say when I was less than willing to go along with her plans. I have wanted to repeat that phrase numerous times when working with an individual who has nothing positive to add and always carries an air of negativity with them. Of course, there is nothing wrong with disagreeing with an idea, but if you disagree, your following sentence should offer a new idea or suggestion.

A negative attitude can halt a career faster than almost any other type of behavior. Unfortunately, research has shown it is easier to be negative and see the downside of events. A poor attitude can manifest in several ways, and as a new manager, it is important to watch for the signs. Some examples include arriving late, carelessly performing tasks, laziness, rudeness to other employees, creating and spreading rumors, naysaying in meetings, or other behaviors that perpetuate a negative environment. A poor attitude can quickly circulate and cause the team environment and motivation to decrease significantly. Each individual is a vital member of the team's success, and when one person is not working effectively, the entire team can struggle to succeed.

LACK OF INITIATIVE

There are no better words to hear from an employee than "I can help with that," "Let me take on that task," or "What can I do to help?" A sure sign of an engaged and motivated employee is initiative. On the opposite end of the spectrum is an employee who lacks initiative and motivation. Employees who don't take the initiative pass up valuable personal and business improvement opportunities that will produce success. They choose to stay in their comfort zone and perform only what is within their scope. These employees drain resources by requiring others to tell them what to do or teach them what they need to know instead of taking the initiative to learn.

THE VICTIM MENTALITY

Employees who play the victim are challenging to work with, as they avoid responsibility in certain aspects of their job. These individuals consistently have scapegoats for their mistakes and display a victim mentality. A victim mentality refers to a state of mind where the person feels the world is against them and nothing is their fault. The victim mentality causes difficult employees to avoid changing, progressing, taking responsibility, and becoming a more significant asset to the company. In turn, they usually underperform and decrease morale.

INABILITY TO DO THEIR JOB

Incompetent employees lack the skills and capabilities needed to succeed in their roles. The inability to do the job may be due to a lack of initiative, lack of prior skills, or lack of motivation. Often, job requirements change, and the difficult employee fails to adapt. The difference in skills required for the job causes the employee to be incompetent in a role that may have previously been a good fit. Excellent employees will quickly update their expertise if the job calls for it. Incompetence can lead to low morale and reduced productivity. Unfortunately, many incompetent employees do not view themselves this way, which makes it difficult to coach them.

ONE NEGATIVE EMPLOYEE CAN IMPACT YOUR TEAM'S PERFORMANCE

Have you ever entered a room where someone is extremely angry or negative? Before you see the person, the tension in the air is palpable. Though it may be on a smaller scale when a team member is negative, it can impact the whole team's performance. This negativity often manifests in complaints about management, workload, or co-workers. It could be gossip about team members or a negative perception of projects or current work. One negative team member can have a catastrophic effect on performance and morale. As a manager, you are responsible for negating negativity and restoring a positive work environment.

Realize the person's concerns may be legitimate. Use active listening skills to understand the root of the negativity. Listen and try to understand the problem and if something can be fixed. There are times when employees are dealing with issues in their personal lives, and due to their struggles, they bring negativity to work. Be a listening ear without condoning the negativity.

Be sure they understand their behavior's effect on the team. Hold them accountable and be clear about the expectations going forward. Be specific in your feedback and understand their boundaries. Employees who feel supported and heard will be less defensive and more open to change.

How to Give Your Employee Difficult Feedback

No manager enjoys telling employees what they are doing wrong or areas they need to improve. However, one of the greatest gifts you can give your employees is honesty and letting them know when they are underperforming and not meeting expectations. It may be difficult, but you are investing in their growth and development as both an individual and an employee.

When we receive negative feedback, we are often thrown into fight, flight, or freeze mode. We may be embarrassed, feel ashamed, get angry, or try to avoid or deny what we are hearing. Neuroscience and psychology research have provided insights into effective ways to deliver difficult feedback.

First, provide facts. Tell them what the exact problem is and leave out any emotion. For example, if an individual is always late turning in work, I suggest you be direct. Make the factual statement as short as possible. The employee may wish to explain or defend themself. Let them know you want to understand the problem, and then discuss it.

Second, share the story of the problem and how their situation affects others. For example, if the employee is consistently turning work in late, it affects others' ability to work and complete their projects. You might say, "When you turn in work after the deadline, it affects the team. Others are delayed starting their portion of the project."

Third, ask for their story and explanation. At this stage, do nothing but listen. Whether the information they share is factual or false doesn't matter. However, they need to share their side of the story, and you might learn something about the individual that will provide insight into why they are underperforming.

Fourth, seek a solution. Ask them how they can solve the problem and how you can help. Give them time (a day or two) to think about a solution. Remember, people change faster and create new habits when they voluntarily choose to and are not forced. Offer suggestions, and if the plan is not robust enough, be honest and help them create a successful strategy.

A strong differentiator between an experienced manager and a new one is how they handle performance reviews with employees. Too often, these reviews are short meetings where managers and employees want to get through the material as quickly as possible and check off the boxes.

Employees want more from their performance reviews. Ninety-six percent of employees reported they want better feedback, and they want it more often. The performance review is a culmination of a year's work and a time to celebrate successes, wins, and personal development, and identify areas for improvement for the upcoming year. It is a disservice to your employees not to provide a performance review that celebrates their hard work and discusses the future.

To ensure a successful performance review, contact your manager, mentor, HR, and other leaders to learn the company's process for conducting performance reviews. Other leaders and your manager will have suggestions and "best practices" they can share to ensure a productive and motivating performance review.

Not all performance reviews are a discussion of wins and successes. Some require candid conversation and difficult feedback. Performance reviews are an excellent opportunity to discuss the individual, what is happening, and how they can improve. These meetings can be a positive first step in helping an employee get back on the right track.

5 Strategies for Managing a Difficult Employee

We have all worked with difficult employees at some point in our careers. Whether it is negative commentary, poor attitude, or incompetence, the problem employee seems to be able to influence any work environment negatively. Therefore, dealing with difficult employees is a guaranteed part of being a manager. Here are five strategies to properly manage difficult employees.

ACTIVELY LISTEN

Managers often err when dealing with problem employees by being too nice, overly critical, or avoiding conflict. Before deciding how to proceed, actively listen and explore what the individual's underlying issue is. Avoid handling difficulties aggressively or sweeping them under the rug. Often, misbehavior is a legitimate concern that is poorly expressed through negative behavior. Instead, ask questions to understand and get a stronger sense of the roots of the behavior. When questions are answered, repeat what you have heard and ask for clarification if the employee needs to feel heard.

CRITIQUE THE BEHAVIOR, NOT THE PERSON

When sharing feedback, critique the behavior and not the person. Criticizing a person, or generalizing inappropriate behavior to their character, can cause defensiveness and distrust. Instead, focus on the acts and the facts. Avoid making assumptions about their motivations ("You are so lazy" or "You enjoy sitting back and letting others do the work") and only comment on the action ("You have not responded to emails promptly or contributed to team meetings"). Instead, communicate calmly and highlight the behavior you wish to be changed. This keeps the conversation clear and actionable.

PROVIDE ACTIONABLE FEEDBACK WITH NEXT STEPS

In *Thanks for the Feedback: The Science and Art of Receiving Feedback Well*, Douglas Stone and Sheila Heen of the Harvard Negotiation Project share that most individuals do not receive feedback well. Instead, criticism may make the employee feel discouraged or defeated. Feedback should include appreciation for what the employee is doing well. Show you recognize the effort they are putting in. Following that, an evaluation of the employee's performance highlights areas of improvement. These should be fact-based and not heavily opinion-driven. Finally, feedback should consist of actionable coaching. Identify the challenges and provide insight into what changes will bring success. Include the employee in developing solutions.

DOCUMENT YOUR CORRESPONDENCE

Human resource experts encourage documenting all correspondence and discussions with difficult employees. Documentation helps support and prove you treated the employees fairly and provided them with opportunities to develop and improve. In addition, documenting a discussion or correspondence will help refute any claims the difficult employee may bring up about being mistreated. Documenting also helps you remain organized in the feedback you have provided and steps the employee should be taking to improve.

FOLLOW UP

Difficult employees will quickly learn if you are involved and committed to their change and development by how often you follow up with them. For example, if you have a discussion with a difficult employee about their performance and do not discuss the issue again for several months, you are sending a message that their performance isn't a priority. Therefore, when managing a difficult employee, it is important to follow up every ten to fourteen business days on their progress and development.

Instances When You Should Involve HR

Human resources departments provide many services to employees and managers. Because you manage people, it is vital to understand when you should alert HR about an event or incident that occurred instead of handling it yourself. Five areas require you to report an incident to HR:

1. An allegation of discrimination, harassment, retaliation, or other unlawful conduct.

2. A request for a leave of absence for medical, family, military, or any other reason.

3. An accommodation request for a physical or emotional condition; a religious belief, practice, or observance; or pregnancy.

4. An allegation that an employee was not properly paid or that their pay was subject to an improper deduction.

5. An employee refuses to perform a task because they believe it is unlawful, unethical, or unsafe.

For each of these areas, you should immediately report the situation to HR when you become aware of it. It does not matter if the employees speak directly to you about the situation in confidence; if you see, hear, or become aware of any of these topics, you must report them. Remember, you cannot ignore any of the above topics, even if no one complains or objects. Speak with your manager and HR representative to get clarification from your organization on each of these topics.

More Often Than Not, Your Employee Wants to Be Successful

During a team lunch, a colleague shared an experience with her first boss: "Straight out of college, I had no experience, and my one qualification was that I was the most eager candidate my boss was interviewing. I had no idea what I wanted to do with my life, but I had a daughter on the way, which lit a fire in me to provide for her needs. I was eager, bordering on desperate. This man took a huge chance on me, as I am sure he interviewed more qualified candidates. He could see my deep desire for success, believing it would translate into a powerful work ethic.

"He hired me and, over the years, became an outstanding mentor who challenged me and set me up to succeed. He had twenty years of experience, knew the industry inside and out, and passed that knowledge on to me. Then, when the time came, he started talking to the right people about me for promotions. This man was the ultimate manager, and I will forever be grateful for his influence and efforts to help me succeed."

Your employees want to succeed. They want to feel good about their work and hope to build a career they are proud of. So, as you manage, always be looking to mentor, guide, and set your team members up for success. Are they promotable? Can you find ways to help them advance or hone skill sets that will make them stand out? Make sure you are on their side and helping them achieve success.

Key Takeaways

The daily work of a manager is challenging, rewarding, and full of learning experiences. In this chapter, you learned tools and tactics to help you successfully develop employees who may not be performing at their best.

→ Great managers identify difficult or poor-performing individuals early and begin coaching and providing feed-back immediately to help their direct reports develop and eventually succeed.

→ Listen to your employees. Ask questions to learn more about why they may be struggling.

→ When providing feedback and coaching, critique the behavior and not the person. Critiquing the individual may cause defensiveness, but focusing on behaviors and actions helps the employee understand how to change and improve.

→ Feedback should include both positive and developmental information. Share what the employee is doing well and provide actionable, clear steps on where and how the employee can improve.

→ Follow up! Always follow up with employees after providing feedback. Find out where they have made progress and where they are still struggling. Allowing too much time to pass before following up signals you are not engaged with the employee's development.

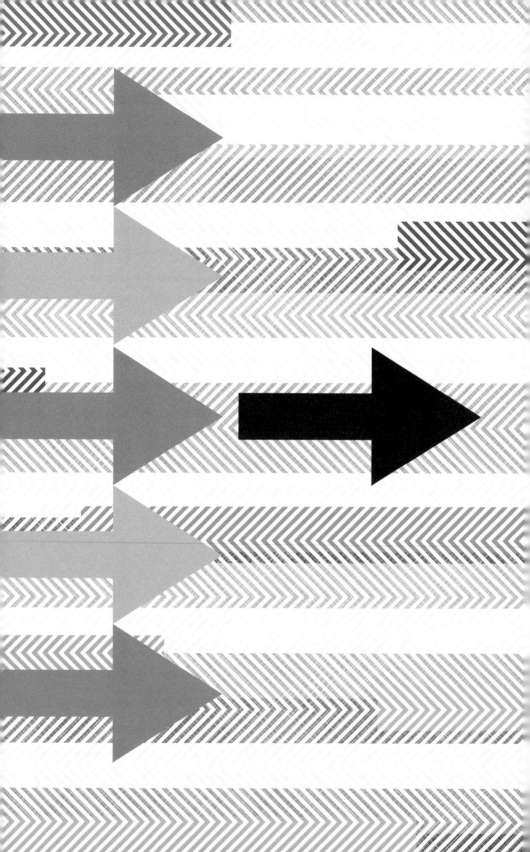

CHAPTER 8

Managing Your Time, Stress, and Growth Potential

Everyone has twenty-four hours in a day. Why is it that some individuals seem to get so much done in a day compared to others? Research into the topic of time management and its effect on stress and peak performance has provided fascinating insights into how the day of a successful manager should be structured.

The first ninety days of being a manager is a busy time. You will be working longer hours as you grasp your new responsibilities and build relationships with direct reports and fellow leaders. Therefore, it is imperative to use the tools, information, and resources discussed in this chapter to maximize your work time, decrease stress, and continue learning and developing in your new role.

This chapter's content and research on managing your day may initially shock you. I highly encourage you to try the tips and tools to see what works best for you. Test and see what works for you and what doesn't. Learn more about managing your time effectively and staying organized while managing stress and work pressure. Using the information in this chapter will help you survive and thrive during a hectic time in your career.

From Burnout to Prioritized Productivity

As I sat across the table from Teresa, it was clear she was exhausted. Sixty days into her role as a new manager, Teresa had been burning the candle at both ends. Learning the team's projects, managing current direct reports, hiring two new individuals, and still finding time to complete her work was wearing her down, both physically and emotionally.

I asked Teresa to describe what was going on. She responded, "I have too much to do and too little time to do it. That is what is going on." The job was managing Teresa; she wasn't managing the position. I asked her to pull out the last month of her calendar so we could review it. Next, I asked her for thirty minutes to organize her next week. She replied, "That is impossible to do." "Let's see what we can do in thirty minutes and go from there." After identifying reoccurring meetings and tasks, we organized her days, starting with her tomorrow. We made a to-do list and then prioritized the activities. We followed up by identifying time-takers she had no control over, such as employee interruptions, phone calls, and Slack messages. After defining which of her activities were top priority, we built in time for interruptions and unexpected requests and even added time for recovery. We finished with an extra forty-five minutes for her to think and plan for the following day. Teresa was amazed as we finished within twenty-five minutes. She was excited and immediately felt relieved. But the essential part of the conversation hadn't occurred yet.

"You have to learn to say no or 'I can in an hour' when any time-takers request your time during other scheduled activities." I explained it was her responsibility to stick (as best she could) to her planned schedule. You must train your team and others; you have a schedule and can make time to talk with them at a later scheduled time. (Unless it is an emergency, of course!) Setting guidelines and boundaries is one of the first steps to positively managing your schedule and reducing stress.

All Managers Make Mistakes

We all make mistakes. Often, it is difficult for a manager to be willing to acknowledge their shortcomings. It takes humility to address your struggles and begin the change process. Managers often wrongly assume that mistakes reflect negatively on them. Conversely, an outstanding manager will acknowledge and take responsibility for their errors, which is an excellent example for employees. It lays the foundation for having a growth mindset on your team. Research has shown those who do not see their abilities as innate or fixed but as something that can be developed through effort tend to achieve more. A mistake does not indicate a lack of ability. It is an opportunity for growth and a stepping-stone for future success. Accepting feedback from others, including those who report to you, demonstrates a willingness to improve.

A manager with a growth mindset will be committed to their employees' development as well as their own. Research has shown that managers with a fixed mindset are less likely to give constructive coaching or feedback to their direct reports. By being willing to see your skill set as a work in progress, you are a better leader and more open to fostering growth in those who report to you.

How to Manage Your Time Effectively

Learning to manage your time effectively will be a career-long endeavor. One day you will feel like you have mastered time management, only to find that the next day your to-do list has grown, deadlines are fast approaching, and you completed half the work you had on your schedule. Learning to manage your time efficiently and effectively can help you stay on track, but this may look different than expected. Managing your time means placing a priority on your time. We often give our time away without considering the value, yet if someone asked us for twenty dollars, we would think twice before handing it to them.

Managing your time means staying organized and knowing your priorities and sticking with them. Managing time means valuing others' time and leading productive and focused meetings. Time management also means having the ability to say no to new requests. For example, when your manager wants to add to your list of projects, the answer may not be a no or yes, but rather, "Which project would you like me to prioritize?" Managing your time is always a work in progress.

STAY ORGANIZED

As a manager, your time is valuable and limited, so always be aware of your priorities. At least once a week, create a list of to-do items and other essential activities and projects so you can keep up with all the demands. This list can be in whatever medium works best for you, whether digitally or with a piece of paper and a pen. Once your priorities are identified, place priority items in your daily schedule. For example, build your day around the most critical items, and then when those are completed, work on less pressing activities. This will help you stay organized.

LEAD PRODUCTIVE MEETINGS

We have all been in unproductive and excessively long meetings. Respect your time and your employees' time by having virtual or in-person meetings that are purposeful, practical, and timely. As obvious as this may sound, first determine if the meeting is necessary. Once you have deemed it important enough for a gathering, create an agenda. Start on time, with no exceptions. Assign time constraints around each topic, so the conversations are not overly lengthy. Send out any information before the meeting so participants can review it before instead of during the meeting. At the end of the meeting, decide on clear action items that require follow-up. The more efficient meetings become, the more time your employees have to create success.

BECOME COMFORTABLE SAYING NO

Saying no to requests can be difficult for new managers, but the ability to say no is crucial for effective time management. Saying no allows you to be deliberate about the activities vital to your success. Unfortunately, the people-pleasing instinct many of us possess may cause us to say yes to others' requests when we do not have the time or bandwidth to help. To increase your ability to say no, avoid an instant answer. Instead, ask questions to understand the request, and then allow yourself time to respond.

DELEGATE

Assert control over your time by delegating. When tasks stack up and become overwhelming, or you do not have time to complete them successfully, use those around you to help. This requires trust in your team. In a leadership role, there is often a desire to take on every task, so it is "done correctly." However, there isn't enough time in the day to complete each task alone, and you may find yourself not meeting deadlines or not doing exemplary work. Delegate so you can focus on higher-level work. To ensure the tasks you delegate are done correctly, provide a clear picture of what must be completed. Choose employees whose skills and traits are most competent for the task.

REJUVENATION AND RECOVERY

An often-forgotten aspect of managing your time effectively is allowing time for rest, rejuvenation, and recovery. Every elite athlete, musician, and corporate leader understands that top performance can only be sustained by prioritizing daily time for rejuvenation and recovery. Schedule a fifteen- to twenty-minute break every two hours so you can move, hydrate, and rest your mind. Research has shown the brain can rarely maintain focused attention for more than 90 to 120 minutes. Therefore, rest breaks are essential every two hours for you to sustain peak performance.

HOW TO DELEGATE SUCCESSFULLY

The initial assumption of a new manager is that delegating benefits only you. In reality, research shows that delegating project tasks and responsibilities, and creative problem-solving, increases productivity, morale, and commitment to the team and the organization. In addition, a 2013 Gallup study showed that leaders who effectively delegate authority grow faster, generate more revenue, and create more jobs. To delegate effectively and successfully, I have included five practices effective leaders use to delegate:

1. Carefully consider the individual to whom you are choosing to delegate. Ensure they have the right skills, capabilities, and interest in a new challenge versus considering only who has the time to complete the project or task.

2. When delegating, be detailed about the expectations and outcome. Have a dialogue to ensure they understand what "success" looks like.

3. Establish specific milestones or check-in points to review the project or task and ensure it is on track.

4. Allow the individual autonomy to accomplish the task. Create an environment that allows them to be creative or add their expertise.

5. Mistakes will always occur. Use these times as a learning tool and development opportunity for your team member.

The ability to delegate successfully is a skill built through practice and repetition. Therefore, delegation is a powerful tool of success for new managers.

Dealing with Criticism or Difficult Feedback

Receiving criticism or negative feedback is difficult. We may go into a fight, flight, or freeze state when we hear negative things about our behavior or traits. We want to belong and be accepted into communities we deem important. So, when we receive criticism or difficult feedback, the first reaction we have assumes that something is wrong with us in an aspect of our life we care about.

One strategy to effectively deal with feedback is to implement a growth mindset, which is a viewpoint that we are getting better and improving throughout our lives. When we receive difficult feedback, we can ask ourselves, "What can I learn from this? What did this experience teach me that I can improve so this doesn't happen again?" Remind yourself, "Mistakes and failures are helping me improve." Managing your perception of the feedback can be a valuable lesson in reaching success.

Another strategy is acknowledging your emotions when receiving criticism and taking them out of the equation. Emotions do not always tell us the truth, especially if they are connected with a fight, flight, or freeze reaction. Acknowledge the feelings you are experiencing and then move away from them into strategic thinking on ways you can implement the criticism or feedback. Allow yourself time to think about the feedback but be careful not to disregard it; use the information to your advantage.

90-DAY TIP: ASK YOUR BOSS FOR FEEDBACK

As a new manager, you mustn't operate in isolation; your success depends on reaching out and actively seeking feedback to improve. Unfortunately, we often don't receive the feedback we need without purposely seeking it out. If you aren't receiving honest feedback, you are missing a vital aspect of your personal growth and development. Feedback will help you meet your goals and avoid putting your prospects for growth at risk.

Research shows that employees who solicit feedback from their managers often are more likely to implement the feedback. Talk with your managers and discuss your desire to receive feedback often. Do not ask at random times without prior notice. The best way is to set up a time with your boss so they can be prepared for the conversation. Ask for ten to fifteen minutes to review your recent performance. Be clear about the three or four specific areas or core competencies you want feedback on. Keep it simple and be open to feedback. Take notes during the meeting and be open to feedback even if you disagree. You may lack insight, and that will take time to think about and understand. Ask for suggestions on ways to improve and then begin putting the feedback into practice.

5 Strategies for Dealing with Stressful Work Situations

Dealing with stressful situations as a new manager is not easy. When you experience stressful work situations, your brain lights up and prepares itself to go into fight, flight, or freeze mode, driven by the sympathetic nervous system. Perhaps your heart is already racing with the natural physiological reaction to stress as you think about it. Creeping deadlines, pressure from senior leaders, and a busy work environment are all factors that cause a manager to be overwhelmed. As the team leader, when those situations undoubtedly arise, the team looks to you for guidance. Stressful situations do not have to be world-altering or devastating. Instead, they can be handled calmly and strategically.

Stressful work situations regularly occur. We will cover strategies to ensure that you can handle stress in a practical, calm, and strategic manner, including taking a moment to process before reacting, addressing what is most urgent, finding opportunities to delegate, getting advice or a second opinion, and building your resilience. Each of these strategies is specifically chosen to help you deal with stress in the workplace.

TAKE A MOMENT TO PROCESS BEFORE REACTING

At work, you will have moments when something does not go as planned, someone gets angry, or an interaction with another employee creates conflict. Remember, human emotion is normal, and everyone has feelings that can be reactive or unkind. Instead of succumbing to the initial automatic responses of fight, flight, or freeze, provide yourself time to process these impulses. These reactive moments are perfect for engaging an internal pause button and taking six deep breaths. Deep breathing counteracts the body's physiological response, summoning your parasympathetic nervous system, which helps return everything to equilibrium. Once you have dealt with the stressful reaction, think and observe the best course of action to take.

ADDRESS WHAT IS MOST URGENT

Successful managers recognize and address what is most urgent in stressful situations. Begin your action plan with the most pressing concern and work from there. If it helps, create a checklist from most to least important. Also, stressful situations are often multifaceted, meaning that stress comes from many different areas. Most of the time, there is a root cause, and other stressors are merely symptoms of a more significant issue. When the immediate fires have been attended to, pinpoint what is causing the stress and attend to that circumstance.

FIND OPPORTUNITIES TO DELEGATE

As a new manager, you want to ensure that your work is always exceptional, which can create excessive stress if you carry a heavy workload. Effective managers identify tasks and strategically and appropriately delegate them when work situations become overwhelming. Strategic delegating includes recognizing the skills and strengths of employees and matching them to the requirements of the job. Do not delegate responsibility to just anyone; this can cause more tension and stress. It is equally important to trust your employees and not micromanage the tasks you have given them.

GET ADVICE OR A SECOND OPINION

One bonus of working in an organization is the number of people around you to draw on for assistance. With different skills and backgrounds, these individuals are a gold mine of advice and opinions that will benefit you. Build a trusted network of colleagues comprising individuals whose judgment you respect. When making decisions about stressful situations, go to these individuals and implement the advice or opinions you deem valuable and relevant. Bouncing ideas and solutions off other people allows you a space to refine and validate these plans.

PRACTICE RESILIENCE AND REDUCING STRESS

There will always be situations at work that cause stress. When these situations occur, whether in your control or not, you must practice resilience techniques to remain at your best. Resilience is the ability to manage, grow and thrive during difficult times. Not only can you practice resilience after stressful situations, but you can also build resilience before difficult events occur to help inoculate yourself against stress and prepare to thrive through difficult times. Choose one activity that enables you to be resilient and put it into practice this week. Some options include breathing techniques, exercise or movement, hobbies, music, or learning something new. Try engaging with these activities a few hours a week to build resilience.

Make Time for Self-Care Outside Work

Jason had been working long hours for more than six months when he decided to take a last-minute vacation. He felt exhausted and worn out and didn't seem able to return to his normal energy levels by relaxing on the weekends. He hoped a short four-day vacation would help. His spouse talked him into a sunrise morning meditation, yoga, and breathing class the hotel offered. After the class, Jason felt like something had unlocked in his brain. He felt calm, energized, and excited for the day, feelings he hadn't felt in the last year. He realized he was not allowing himself time to care for himself outside work, to increase his resilience and reduce stress.

Every high-level athlete, musician, and artist understands that rest, rejuvenation, and self-care are just as important as practicing. Rest and rejuvenation allow the brain to recover and input information learned during practice. Recovery also allows for increased creativity and the enjoyment of hobbies or other activities that bring joy and happiness to our lives. Unfortunately, we live in a society that emphasizes never-ending work, but a whole life incorporates hard work *and* time to relax and enjoy hobbies and friends.

The Most Important Key to Success: Never Stop Learning

Based on my observations and experience, the key to a fulfilling life and career is to never stop learning. Highly successful people in every type of work know that continual learning and development promotes success and fulfillment. Find anyone in business who is respected and admired, and you will see a life of constant learning, study, growth, and curiosity. At its core, curiosity and lifelong learning is the skill of finding ways to improve constantly. The best companies spend millions on training and improving the skills of their employees. They understand the power of investing in the personal growth of their workforce.

The best way to learn is to start small. If you don't usually read a ton of books, don't set a goal to read fifty books a year. Set small, achievable goals. Read one book this month. Find something that interests you and dig into it. Look at your position in the company from a new angle and find ways to improve how you lead and work. You make yourself irreplaceable to the organization by constantly striving to be better. Be the best at what you do.

Because you are more than your career, it is essential to note research has shown that setting goals create a happier, more fulfilling life overall. People are happier if they are progressing and proud of the life they have built. You are creating a well-rounded, happy life by being a lifelong learner. Start learning something today!

Key Takeaways

The first ninety days of being a manager are full of new experiences and learning opportunities. As a new manager, managing your time, stress, and personal development is crucial to your success and impact on your employees. Learning to manage your time effectively will be a career-long endeavor. There will be times you master time management, and at other times you will feel disorganized and overwhelmed. Be patient with yourself as you learn and apply new skills, because every new manager makes mistakes as they learn a new position.

→ To manage your time effectively, stay organized. Keep track of daily meetings and commitments. Keep a list of priority projects and individuals.

→ Build your day around the most critical items and projects to complete. Don't put off working on what is important until the end of the day. Instead, do vital work when your mind is alert and ready to work.

→ Delegate projects and items to others so you can focus on higher-level tasks and develop your team's capabilities and skills.

→ Deal with stressful work situations by taking a moment to pause before reacting. Allow time to think about what you will say and how you respond to others. Then, if needed, seek advice or a second opinion.

A FINAL NOTE

Congratulations on finishing this book and striving to be an effective and influential manager. Your desire to improve your management skills will pay off as you continue your leadership journey. I hope you look back over your first ninety days as a leader with a sense of pride and relief. You did it! You now have relationships in place, processes implemented, and a sense of who you are as a leader and what you want to accomplish. You are also well equipped to handle the hurdles and stumbling blocks that may come your way.

As you begin the next phase of your leadership journey, be sure to focus on your learning and development, and the development of your team members. This focus will put you and your team on track to be peak performers. My last advice is always remember you are on a leadership journey. As the workplace changes, the world changes, your products change, and possibly the organization you work for changes, you will have ups and downs in your career. You will have incredible successes, failures, and hardships. But they are only small stops on a lifelong journey. I wish you success and hope this book will help make your journey a bit easier.

RESOURCES

Apps

LinkedIn: A social network that focuses on professional networking and career development. You can use LinkedIn to display your résumé, search for jobs, and enhance your professional reputation by posting updates and interacting with other business leaders.

Mind Tools: The Mind Tools app provides access to a wide selection of bite-size, career-enhancing resources, so you can build vital skills wherever and whenever it suits you. In addition, the app is full of information for new leaders in a quickly consumable format.

Books

Bonds That Make Us Free: Healing Our Relationships, Coming to Ourselves, by C. Terry Warner: Suggests that personal transformations occur when you reflect on your relationships with fresh honesty. This self-reflection lifts you from negative thoughts and feelings toward others and helps you empathize and better understand others.

Bringing Up the Boss: Practical Lessons for New Managers, by Rachel Pacheco: Using anecdotes and research, the author shares tools and how-tos that quickly help new employees become expert managers.

Crucial Conversations: Tools for Talking When Stakes Are High, by Kerry Patterson, Joseph Grenny, Ron McMillan, Al Switzler, and Emily Gregory: Teaches managers and employees how to remain calm and get the results you want when conflict emerges. With the skills you learn in this book, you'll never have to worry about the outcome of a crucial conversation again.

Dare to Lead: Brave Work. Tough Conversations. Whole Hearts., by Brené Brown: Research, stories, and examples in the no-nonsense style millions of readers have come to expect and appreciate.

HBR's 10 Must Reads for New Managers. This is a collection of ideas and best practices for aspiring and experienced leaders alike, helping individuals transition from being outstanding individual contributors to becoming great managers of others. If you read nothing else on becoming a new manager, read this book.

Periodicals

Harvard Business Review (HBR.com): This is the leading destination for management thinking and solutions. It aims to provide professionals worldwide with rigorous insights and best practices to help lead themselves and their organizations more effectively. Find new ideas and classic advice on strategy, innovation, and leadership.

MIT Sloan Management Review (SloanReview.MIT.edu): Explore how leadership and management are transforming in a disruptive world. The *MIT Sloan Management Review* helps thoughtful leaders learn skills and capabilities to become influential managers while facing the challenges created as technological, societal, and environmental forces reshape how organizations operate, compete, and create value.

Podcasts

The Dr. CK Bray Show: Author's podcast. Provides information you need to create a better life, be a better leader, and further your career. The more than 450 episodes provide listeners with advice and tools.

Jocko Podcast: Retired Navy SEAL Jocko Willink and producer Echo Charles discuss discipline and leadership in business, relationships, and everyday life.

Manager Tools: A weekly business podcast focused on helping professionals become more effective managers and leaders. It shares specific actions and tools that help professionals achieve their desired management and career objectives.

TED Business: Host Modupe Akinola of Columbia Business School presents powerful and surprising ideas illuminating the business world. After the talk, you'll get a mini lesson on how to apply the ideas in your own life.

Websites

edX.org: edX is a mission-driven, massive open online course (MOOC) provider. They partner with leading universities and organizations to offer high-quality online courses to learners worldwide. In addition, edX offers courses in management, leadership, and human behavior.

ManagerTools.com: A website for both new and experienced managers. Its mission is to make every manager effective. In addition, they have a free weekly newsletter and podcast designed to give managers actionable recommendations in all areas of leadership.

ScienceOfPeople.com: Learn science-based communication tips that uncover the hidden forces that drive our behavior. Great for new leaders, this website offers insight into human behavior at work.

REFERENCES

"2020 Workplace Learning Report." LinkedIn Learning. Accessed October 3, 2022. learning.linkedin.com/resources/workplace -learning-report-2020.

Abramovich, Giselle. "If You Think Email Is Dead, Think Again." September 8, 2019. *Adobe Blog*. blog.adobe.com/en/publish/ 2019/09/08/if-you-think-email-is-dead-think-again.

Agrawal, Sapana, Aaron De Smet, Sébastien Lacroix, and Angelika Reich. "To Emerge Stronger from the COVID-19 Crisis, Companies Should Start Reskilling Their Workforces Now." May 7, 2020. McKinsey & Company. mckinsey.com/capabilities/ people-and-organizational-performance/our-insights/ to-emerge-stronger-from-the-covid-19-crisis-companies -should-start-reskilling-their-workforces-now.

Amabile, Teresa, and Steven Kramer. *The Progress Principle: Using Small Wins to Ignite Joy, Engagement, and Creativity at Work*. Grand Haven, MI: Brilliance Audio, 2012.

Belk Olson, Andrea. "4 Common Reasons Strategies Fail." *Harvard Business Review*. June 24, 2022. hbr.org/2022/06/4-common -reasons-strategies-fail.

Chui, Michael, James Manyika, Jacques Bughin, Richard Dobbs, Charles Roxburgh, Hugo Sarrazin, Geoffrey Sands, and Magdalena Westergren. "The Social Economy: Unlocking Value and Productivity through Social Technologies." McKinsey Global Institute. July 1, 2012. mckinsey.com/ industries/technology-media-and-telecommunications/ our-insights/the-social-economy.

Clear, James. *Atomic Habits: Tiny Changes, Remarkable Results*. New York: Avery, 2018.

Engel, Jacob M. "Why Does Culture 'Eat Strategy for Breakfast'?" *Forbes*. November 20, 2018. forbes.com/sites/forbescoaches council/2018/11/20/why-does-culture-eat-strategy-for -breakfast/?sh=124f01b81e09.

Fidler, Devin. *"Future Skills*: Update + Literature Review." Institute for the Future for ACT Foundation and the Joyce Foundation. 2016. iftf.org/futureskills.

Galbraith, Morgan. "Don't Just Tell Employees Organizational Changes Are Coming—Explain Why." *Harvard Business Review*. October 5, 2018. hbr.org/2018/10/dont-just-tell -employees-organizational-changes-are-coming -explain-why.

Goerg, Sebastian J. "Goal Setting and Worker Motivation." *IZA World of Labor*, vol. 178 (2015). wol.iza.org/articles/goal -setting-and-worker-motivation.

Goleman, Daniel. "What Makes a Leader?" *Harvard Business Review*. January 2005. hbr.org/2004/01/what-makes-a-leader.

The Harvard Business Review Manager's Handbook: The 17 Skills Leaders Need to Stand Out. Boston: Harvard Business Review Publishing, 2017.

Hidayat, Rahmat, and Jaka Budiatma. "Education and Job Train-ing on Employee Performance." *International Journal of Social Sciences and Humanities* 2, no. 1 (April 2018): 171–81. doi.org/10.29332/ijssh.v2n1.140.

Hill, Linda A. "New Manager Development for the 21st Century." *Academy of Management Executive* 18, no. 3 (August 2004): 121–26. www.hbs.edu/faculty/Pages/item.aspx?num=17972.

Hogan, Robert, and Rodney Warrenfeltz. "Educating the Modern Manager." *Academy of Management Learning & Education* 2, no. 1 (March 2003): 74–84. jstor.org/stable/40214169.

"Jabra Hybrid Ways of Working: 2021 Global Report." Jabra. August 2021. jabra.com/hybridwork.

Mahan, Thomas F., Danny Nelms, Jeeun Yi, Alexander T. Jackson, Michael Hein, and Richard Mofett. "2020 Retention Report." Work Institute. Franklin, TN: Work Institute, 2020. info.workinstitute.com/hubfs/2020%20Retention%20Report/ Work%20Institutes%202020%20Retention%20Report.pdf.

Marcus for Business. "What People/Process/Product Means & How It Can Help Your Business." Marcus Lemonis. Accessed October 3, 2022. marcuslemonis.com/business/3ps-of -business.

The Radicati Group. "Email Statistics Report, 2021–2025." February 2021. radicati.com/wp/wp-content/uploads/2021/ Email_Statistics_Report,_2021-2025_Executive_Summary.pdf.

"re:Work Guide: Understand Team Effectiveness." Google. Accessed September 26, 2022. rework.withgoogle.com/print/ guides/5721312655835136.

"State of the Global Workplace, 2013." Gallup. Accessed September 28, 2022. gallup.com/topic/state-of-the-global-workplace -2013.aspx.

"State of the Global Workplace, 2023." Gallup. Accessed September 28, 2022. gallup.com/workplace/349484/state-of-the-global -workplace-2022-report.aspx.

Stone, Douglas, and Sheila Heen. *Thanks for the Feedback: The Science and Art of Receiving Feedback Well*. New York: Penguin Books, 2015.

Toegel, Ginka, and John-Louis Barsoux. "How to Become a Better Leader." *MIT Sloan Management Review* 53, no. 3 (March 2012): 51. sloanreview.mit.edu/article/how-to-become -a-better-leader.

Zak, Paul J. "The Neuroscience of Trust." *Harvard Business Review* (January–February 2017). hbr.org/2017/01/the -neuroscience-of-trust.

INDEX

A

active listening skills, 20, 108
adaptability, 13
advice, seeking, 124, 127
Amabile, Teresa, 24
appearance, professional, 20
arrogance, 39
Atomic Habits (Clear), 87
attitude, negative, 103, 105
authenticity, 43
autonomy, promoting, 45, 78

B

balance sheets, 90
biases, 74
bosses
  clashing with, 56
  learning from ineffective,
    61–62
  learning working style of,
    54–55, 59–60
  managing up, 50, 59–61, 63
  presenting strategic plans
    to, 94
  requesting feedback from, 122
  responsibilities to, 51
  working with, 52–54, 63
Brailsford, David, 83–84
brain
  challenges and, 45
  fight, flight, or freeze mode,
    106, 121, 123
  reward state, 19

stress and, 123
uncertainty and, 21
brainstorming, 93
breathing exercise, 123
burnout, 116
business
  company culture, 36, 47, 92
  company goals, 84–85
  financials, understanding,
    89–90
  organizational strategy, 92
  three Ps of, 5–7, 15
  understanding critical areas
    of, 8

C

career development, 78–79
cash flow statements, 90
challenges, attainable, 45
change
  embracing, 15
  managing through, 21
  resistance to, 102
  VUCA nature of, 13
Clear, James, 87
collaboration, 57–58, 79, 94
commitment, to keeping your
    word, 44
communication
  with bosses, 52, 60–61
  built via trust, 35
  as a daily responsibility, 9, 10

disorganized/opaque/
dishonest, 38
lack of regular, 38
nonverbal, 20
strong skills, 19
company culture, 36, 47, 92
compassion, 27, 28
compounded action, 87
confidence, demonstrating, 20
COVID-19 pandemic, 13, 38
criticism, 44, 109, 112, 121.
See also feedback
customers, meeting needs of, 7

D

deadlines, meeting, 51
delegation, 119, 120, 124, 127
deliverables, monitoring, 11
direct reports. *See also*
    employees; team members
    maintaining professionalism
    with, 25
    one-on-ones with, 21, 42,
    70–71
    supporting, 21
dishonesty, 38
distrust, reasons for, 37–39, 47
documentation, importance
    of, 109
dopamine, 10
Drucker, Peter, 36

E

Edelman Trust Barometer, 35
email, as a daily responsibility, 9
emotions, acknowledging, 121
empathy, 27

employees. *See also* direct
    reports; team members
    achieving success, 46, 47,
    101, 111
    communicating with, 10
    difficult, 102–105, 108–109
    goal-setting, 10
    hiring, 12
    motivating, 18
    providing feedback to, 10, 12,
    106, 108–109, 112
    role of in process analysis, 7
    terminating, 12
    training, 11
    trust in, 6
    underperforming, 74–75, 100
engagement, 39
external business factors, 92
eye contact, 20

F

fairness, 39
feedback
    asking bosses for, 122
    being unreceptive to, 24
    to bosses, 60–61
    as a daily responsibility, 9, 12
    difficult, giving, 106, 108–109
    difficult, receiving, 121
    following up, 109, 112
    performance reviews, 107
    praise, 44
    to team members, 73
financials, importance of
    understanding, 89–90
following up, 109, 112

taking responsibility for, 117
motivation
  bosses,' 54
  employee, 18, 21, 46
  increased via trust, 35
  lack of, 39

N

negativity, in employees,
    103, 105
networking, 58, 124
"no," saying, 119
nonverbal communication, 20

O

observation
  of bosses, 59–60
  of team members, 72–73
organizational strategy, 92
ownership, sense of, 78

P

peers, managing former, 41
peer-to-peer learning, 78
people, as essential to
    success, 6
performance reviews, 107.
    See also feedback
posture, confident, 20
praise, 44
prioritization, 118
processes
  essential to success, 6, 7
  understanding, 75–76
productivity
  impact of poor management
    on, 26

increased via trust, 35
products, as essential to
    success, 6, 7
professional appearance, 20
The Profit (TV show), 6
progress monitoring, 11

R

rapport, creating, 43–45
recognition, 44
recovery, 119, 125–126
rejuvenation, 119, 125–126
relationships
  with bosses, 49–56
  with employees, 25, 28, 41,
    70–71
  with other managers, 57–58
resiliency, 125
respect, from employees, 24
responsibilities
  day-to-day, 9–12, 15
  evolving, 13
  role alignment with, 77
rest breaks, 119, 125–126
roadblocks, change as, 21

S

satisfaction, job, 35
second opinions, seeking, 124,
    127
self-assessment, 77
self-awareness, 43
self-care, 119, 125–126
Stone, Douglas, 109
strategic plans
  creating, 91–93, 95
  drafting, 93–94

Acknowledgments

This book has been enjoyable to write as I look back over my career journey. I must thank all the leaders over the years who provided excellent examples of how to lead and influence others. Most important, thank you to my family, who allow me quiet time to think and write. Thanks to my incredible wife, Gale, who read the entire manuscript several times to ensure my words conveyed what I wanted—all while finishing up and graduating with her master's degree from Harvard. I couldn't have finished this book in the short window I did without my daughter Olivia. She read, edited, and provided excellent insights about management from the Gen Z perspective. She is one smart, witty, and incredible writer. One day you will be reading her books! Also, Chloe, Elle, Bryson (welcome to the family), Ava, Eve, and Crew. Family is what life is all about.

About the Author

Dr. CK Bray is a cognitive-behavioral researcher, speaker, author, and CEO/founder of the Adaption Institute, a research-based firm that provides science-based solutions for organizations. He graduated from the University of Oklahoma with a PhD in organizational and adult development and is ABD for a second PhD in industrial/organizational psychology with a concentration in the cognitive sciences. CK also earned an MBA. He is a researcher and faculty member at the Harvard Brain Health Initiative. His first book, *Best Job Ever!*, was a *USA Today* best-seller, and his second, *How to Raise Remarkable Kids Without Talking to Them*, was released in December 2021. He resides in Arizona with his wife and six children. He is an ice cream connoisseur, tennis and pickleball fanatic, and ten years (eight thousand hours) away from being a concert pianist.